THE AUTOBIOGRAPHY
of a sex worker

Nalini Jameela

TRANSLATED AND WITH A FOREWORD BY

J. Devika

Westland ltd

westland ltd
61, Silverline Building, Alapakkam Main Road, Maduravoyal, Chennai 600 095
No. 38/10 (New No.5), Raghava Nagar, New Timber Yard Layout, Bangalore 560 026
93, 1st Floor, Sham Lal Road, Daryaganj, New Delhi 110 002

First published in Malayalam by DC Books
First published in English by westland ltd 2007

ISBN: 978-81-89975-11-1

Cover Illustration: Rahul Sharma

Typeset in ITC Legacy Sans Std by Ram Das Lal

Printed at Anubha Printers

Contents

INTRODUCTION

I Try Out Writing

It was in 2001 that I decided to write an autobiography. This decision had a context. I had this habit: whenever I spoke, I would slip into descriptions of my own life quite unwittingly, and go on and on. And people like Paulson and Maitreyan, my colleagues at Jwalamukhi, would often ask me, why stop with this chatter, why not write it all up as a story? Paulson was the one who wanted the story; Maitreyan suggested I write an autobiography. To tell you the truth, I didn't have a clue about the difference between the two.

Then once, during a discussion about a video workshop at Maitreyan's house, he told me again: 'You should definitely write your autobiography, you should!' I said, that's tough for me. It's difficult for me to write. Just when I manage to pick up speed in writing, a letter goes missing. And when I ferret out the letter, the idea I was trying to express has vanished. That was the trouble, in the first place.

The suggestion, however, was put to me many times, and it was in 2003 that I finally decided to write the autobiography. During a discussion about organising the 'Festival of Pleasure', Rajasekharan, a member of our support group (he works for the magazine *Savvy*), gave me a tip about how to write an autobiography: write one page every day, he said. I could get up early in the morning and write. Short notes would do for a start. Later, we could have someone expand them.

I did try to start as he had advised many times, but I couldn't move beyond a few sentences. 'I am Nalini. Was born at Kalloor near Amballoor. I am forty-nine years old.' I wrote this much in a notebook. And then a client happened to read this. That led to my losing him. I'd told him that I was only forty-two! My first attempts to write were blocked by this incident.

After this, I got a school child to write for me, while I was at Beemappalli. That kid used to read *Mangalam* and *Manorama*, magazines that lots of people read. But nothing worthwhile came out of this. And so it was also given up.

By this time, many people had heard I was planning to write my autobiography. So I. Gopinath approached me in 2004 at the Kerala Social Forum at Thrissur and offered to write my autobiography by taking down what I told him. I agreed, and in a year's time, we had more than twelve very detailed interviews on tape. Unfortunately, many of those cassettes were lost and he had to rely on his memory to rewrite most parts.

In our eagerness to see the book published, we did not give ourselves enough time to make it perfect. That's why I decided to write a revised autobiography.[1] A group of friends

---

[1] The first version was Nalini Jameela, *Oru Laingikatozhilaliyute Atmakatha* (Autobiography of a Sex Worker), Kottayam: DC Books, 2005. This went into six editions in one hundred days, and sold 13,000 copies.

volunteered to revise it keeping my style intact. I'm truly grateful to them — they've put in such hard work — and to Gopinath who helped me to shape my autobiography into a book for the first time.

Many asked me if it was right to make such revisions. I don't know if there are rules about these things that apply to everyone around the world. Even if there are, and I happen to be the first person to change those rules, let it be so! After all, when I started sex work, I didn't go by custom! When I spoke with the publisher, Ravi D.C., he agreed to bring out the revised edition. I want to do everything to make my autobiography match my standards and style. I'm thankful to everyone who has helped me. Special thanks to Gita Krishnankutty, for reading this book and suggesting changes.

−*Nalini Jameela*

TRANSLATOR'S FOREWORD
Nalini Jameela Writes Her Story

Nalini Jameela came into public view in Kerala in 2005 when her autobiography, *Oru Laingikatozhilaliyute Atmakatha,* was published in Malayalam, and became a controversial bestseller. The book went into six editions in one hundred days and sold 13,000 copies. No less an authority than M. Mukundan, one of Kerala's most powerful literary figures, condemned the book as a 'prurient money-spinner'. The controversy deepened when Jameela decided to reject the first version, and prepare a second version, which she authorised as the authentic one.

The furious debate around the book and its author, in which 'inadvertent alliances' between voices from the conservative right and some feminists were formed, evoked memories of an earlier controversy over a woman writing her story. This was in the early 1970s, and the controversy had been about the 'revealing' autobiography written by one of Kerala's finest literary authors, Madhavikutty (Kamala Das). However, no two authors could be so differently located. Madhavikutty was born into an aristocratic Nair family, was the daughter of an eminent poet in Malayalam, and the niece of a prominent intellectual. She was already well known as a short story writer in Malayalam and as a poet and writer in English when *Ente Katha* appeared. Jameela came from a lower-middle class, lower caste (Ezhava) family, was removed from school at nine, and worked as a labourer and a domestic worker before becoming a sex worker. Later she became an activist and a filmmaker, but was not very well known outside a narrow sphere.

Now it seemed as if she had taken over the crown of thorns from Madhavikutty — who had once been disparagingly referred to as the 'queen of erotica'. There were further differences: Madhavikutty chose to withdraw her controversial autobiography after many years of struggle, calling it a 'fictional account'; Jameela chose to reclaim her autobiography by producing a second version which she felt was satisfactory. She risked commercial failure and public disapproval in order to 'correct' her image. For Jameela, a successful autobiography was her way of establishing herself as a public person, while testifying to the oppression of sex workers in public. She could not simply withdraw the first version; she had to rewrite it.

What was striking about the debate, however, was that it failed to recognize the fundamental challenge the book had raised to the dominant feminine ideal in Kerala. This ideal of the procreative, disciplined, family-centred feminine, enshrined within the Malayali new elite, had taken shape through wave after wave of social and community reformism in the 20th century. *Oru Laingikatozhilaliyute Atmakatha* exploded this ideal, appearing as an oppositional voice in the Malayali public. The Veshya — the prostitute-figure — was marginally present in early 20th century Malayali reformist discussions on the shaping of modern Womanhood as its abhorrent Other. However, the poor labouring women's presence was even more marginal. Jameela's text actually made this voice audible.

Like the *Bhrtya,* the female labourer of the classical Sanskritic typology, the narrator of this story performs *different kinds of labour* — productive, reproductive, sexual. Indeed, Jameela indicates that sex workers are an unstable group. One reason why her work appeared shocking was that it challenged dominant images of decay as the inevitable culmination of a 'sinful life'. Instead, it highlighted the ordinariness of sex work in the lives of the poorest women, its place alongside other strenuous, exploitative and demeaning work — situations quite invisible to Kerala's educated elite. That the boundaries dividing workplace, home and the place of sexual labour are quite unclear emerges in Jameela's insight that the threat of sexual violence is equally forbidding in all these disparate work places. About her initiation into sex work, she says: 'The moment she mentioned "needing women" I understood that this had to do with using the woman the way the husband does.'

Jameela's autobiography reveals the exclusions of the dominant home-centred, self-controlled feminine ideal and challenges the prostitute-stereotype. In her very title, she calls herself a *laingikatozhilali,* a sex worker, claiming the dignity of *tozhil,* a word that can mean both 'labour' and 'profession' in Malayalam. Jameela does not seek *direct* entry to elite Womanhood. She rejects the description of herself as a 'prostitute' as defined by the forces of morality — but this is not done so that she can claim a description that would situate her in the community of 'Women'. That she chooses a description defined by labour indicates the distance between elite-centred notions of 'Womanhood' and the female labouring poor in Kerala.

Jameela's jettisoning of the anonymity that helps her in her work upsets stereotypical expectations regarding biographical writing by sex workers. She mentions in her introduction that her attempts to note down personal details ended in her losing a client once he learned her real age!

Thirdly, Jameela inserts a 'domestic' into her life-narrative, complicating the image of the 'public woman' considerably. Stereotypically, domestic rhythms, familial love and relation-ships are perceived to be absent from the life of the sex worker (a 'public woman') — her life is expected to be essentially a series of sexual adventures.

Yet Jameela's narrative has no explicit descriptions of sex; when it is discussed, she employs amusing analogies. She includes a series of stories about being a wife, mother and devoted member of her husband's family, long accounts of her relatives by marriage, her daughter's marriages and her son-in-law. But the foregrounding of the domestic here does not obscure the 'public life' that Jameela states as her choice within given circumstances; nor does it idealize the domestic or conceal the tensions of negotiating between the two. Next,

Jameela does link sex work to the production of pleasure and beauty — however, through her characterisation of sex work as 'counselling' and 'therapy', and claims to possessing 'expertise', she appropriates the former into the latter. And when Jameela advocates difference rather than sameness between the sexes, it is on entirely different ground.

In short, Jameela's autobiography rejects dominant Womanhood not only by relating the hitherto-untold story of the marginalized labouring woman-subject, but also by not seeking to be defined within the home-centred category of Women. Indeed, she seeks a revaluation of sex work as a 'professional activity', thus bidding for a public, knowledge-based identity. Jameela also upsets stereotypes and complicates the boundaries between the Domestic Woman and her Other by 'writing in' an elaborate domestic into her narrative. Central to this text is the figure of the Public Woman, who is clearly distant from the dominant domestic ideal, but also lives a domestic life, and aspires for the (largely masculine) role of the knowledgeable 'expert'.

Pride, Prejudice, and Worse

Jameela's entry into the public world was through the re-organising of sex workers by NGOs as part of the AIDS prevention campaigns. Sex workers began to assert themselves publicly, for instance, when the Malayalam film *Susanna* (2001) was released. Indeed, the sex workers' identification with *Susanna* seems linked to the fact its chief protagonist is highly endowed with Womanly qualities and engages in multi-partner relationships — making a bid for inclusion. The emerging differences between the sex workers and prominent feminists/radicals were already apparent, and would worsen later.

Jameela's feminist critics regard her narrative as the neo-liberal *Veshya's* voice. Certainly, Jameela's liberalist pronouncements on sex work, the liberal disembodied self that underpins it and her 'male sexual need' argument may be critiqued. But the anti-patriarchal charge in defining the prostitute as a radically disembodied ego, as not just a body, but its owner, cannot be simply denied. Critics often imply that Jameela is *essentially* a saleable body masquerading as the owner of one. Her salvation from bodily-ness, then, lies in a variant of reformism, in rescue and rehabilitation that would transform her into a mind-centred Woman under the supervision of superior 'minds', possibly feminists: hence the heavy moralism of Jameela's feminist opponents. Nor do they reflect on why commercial domestic work, which is equally exploitative, onerous and sometimes involves bodily services, does not carry social stigma.

Jameela has appeared as a 'victim', as a passive tool in the hands of neo-liberal reformers; in contrast, liberals have emphasized her 'agency'. This allowed for the obscuring of the voice of the *Bhrtya*, who is neither the ideal Woman, nor her Other — the Prostitute — but a third, for whom either of these terms or their opposition makes sense. The unflinching focus on Jameela's sex work obscured her class position as a poor labouring woman. For instance, researchers have observed that poor, labouring women in Kerala increasingly work harder to 'marry off' daughters with substantial dowries, perceiving this as a survival strategy in the face of direct capitalist oppression. Jameela's own attempts to 'marry off' her daughter has close similarities with such attitudes.

The constant accusation made by her critics in their zeal to depict Jameela as an 'unrepentant sex trader' willing to 'let her daughter pursue sex work if she chose it' obscured her challenge to the prostitute-stereotype. It ignores her admission of intolerable working conditions in sex work and her reluctance to encourage her daughter to take up sex work. It was never conceded by her critics that the conceptual and moral oppositions that structure elite society may not make sense to the non-elite. Jameela's statement continued to be read within those very oppositions. The key — and incorrect — implication was that Jameela allows her family to be open to sex trade — and therefore her claims to be part of the domestic are annulled. The statement attributed to her had been culled from her replies in a question-and-answer pamphlet published by the Sex Workers' Forum in 2003, which was clearly impatient, if not dismissive, of the socialist critique of globalisation. Interestingly, this has been appended to the first version of her autobiography (which she subsequently rejected) to achieve a seamless unity between her life and the Sex Workers' Forum's political statements, in effect effacing her as an individual and a writer.

In addition, the debate obliterated a valuable, implicit point in her account of the changing institutional arrangements of sex work — that it is as varied and historically evolved in Malayali society as are family ties. Again, her work has been condemned as 'prurient literature' — neo-liberal contagion. Mukundan's tirade against Jameela reveals how misogyny can be passed off as moral outrage against 'bad women', in this case disguised as concern about Malayali reading habits. He laments that the future best-seller will not be 'written by a great (male) author (*ezhuttukaaran*) of our language, but by a sex worker or (female) sex trafficker (*penvanibhakkari*)'.

The political implications of Jameela's pointing to the possibility of sex workers becoming 'experts' in sex therapy may be missed in the near-hysterical chorus that sees this as evidence for her advocacy of a sex tourism industry. Yet her rooting of this claim in 'subjugated knowledges' gained in the course of life as a sex worker rather than in knowledge acquired through institutions definitely has other implications.

Lastly, some interesting self-contradictions in the text were ignored. For instance, Jameela implies that sex work can include the offering of affection and warmth, for instance, in the claim that sex workers are trying to create 'a collective of friends who love each other' and not 'husbands and wives who torture each other'. Yet in other cases, she hints that this may be difficult. She once mentions falling in love with a client. It is significant that pleasure for her begins with his recognition of her as *a person*, through sight, through the face beyond blind touch. This, it seems, is what makes sex with him non-alienating. But for reformer-intellectuals, this is evidence for either her dishonesty or non-rigorous thinking. This apparently leaves untouched their neat constructions of Nalini Jameela as the very embodiment of the liberal position on sex work.

Indeed, her autobiography is certainly no flawless neo-liberal text. The many 'slips' in Jameela's recent text thwart homogenising or essentialising descriptions. First, despite the fact that Jameela's opinions about the nature and conditions of sex work have been shaped within a liberal understanding, the narration of experiences as sex worker upturn these, bringing into view the undeniably exploitative conditions under which sex work is actually carried out. Indeed, through this very narration she resists mocking or infantilising the client, even claiming a pedagogic relationship with him. When she speaks of her own ways of working, she spells out the 'limits' she has set to her liberalism. Further, she claims to be '...insistent that I wouldn't wiggle my hips and arms to catch anyone; the client had to come to me'. She does not offer a homogenized image of the 'sex worker' presented, though she does use it in specific contexts elsewhere. In her narration, the constraints that shape her agency are amply visible. Indeed, the lack of the 'freedom to refuse', which she identifies as a key component of the sex worker's 'free' existence, is often implicitly admitted.

Connections and Non-connections

As a feminist historian, I was initially attracted to Jameela's challenge to entrenched gender ideals in Kerala, the history of which I have traced in my own work. But as a feminist I was drawn to her remarkable combination of skills: a remarkable ability to argue rationally, and an uncanny eye for analogy and metaphor, all drawn from the ordinary materials of everyday life. Indeed, she reminded me of the Buddhist nun, Punna, the wise *dasi*, of the *Therigatha*, who reminded the brahmin that one cannot acquire spiritual merit through bathing in the Ganga, for if this were so, then the fish, the tortoises and all the other creatures that live in the river would go straight to heaven! Punna's capacity for rational thinking, combined with her observations in her extremely trying everyday existence as a *dasi*, grows into an argument against the superstition of the holy dip.

As a translator, I struggled to retain the complexities of the argument — in which a neoliberal political language often jostled for space with contrary positions — as well as Jameela's personal writing style. Jameela's meandering, casually conversational manner, her method of suddenly bringing the ironic laughter of resistance right into the middle of descriptions of shocking oppression, had to be transferred carefully. Her trick of discussing past events in the present tense was, however, difficult to retain. Also, while Jameela follows a broadly linear narrative, she often digresses into the past, and moves into the future. Most of these shifts have been retained in this text, with a few exceptions in which the jump appeared too awkward and disruptive to retain. As she herself mentions in the interview appended, the last chapter is not really a last chapter at all.

However, my decision to translate the book — made in the spirit of friendship — was not an easy one, given the fact that none other than prominent Malayali feminists led the trenchant attack on Jameela's writing. These feminist activists had little in common with me, though I too lay claim to that label. In effect, these middle class new-elite feminists claimed, in extraordinarily shrill voices, that if Jameela refused victim status, she must truly be a social scourge: for prostitutes, unless they are repentant, must certainly be social scourges. One key difference between me as a feminist and other feminists was our very different positioning vis-à-vis the institution of marriage. Some of the latter drew directly or indirectly on their respectably-married, matronly status, blithely assuming that their success in forming less oppressive families was not really connected to their advantageous social and economic position. In doing so, they projected themselves as fully within the dominant — but able to transform it in their own terms — and thus entitled to launch a moralistic tirade.

My strategy, however, has been to stay outside marriage, and to set up claims to the familial outside it, and thus draw up an alternate model. Perhaps my 'inadvertent alliances' are not so much with respectable feminists, as with the abject, including sex workers! Nevertheless, I am aware of what separates me from Jameela — my sticking within my elite social circle, my kin network, 'respectable', if not conjugal, domestic arrangements, educational and career achievements — these are the unstated advantages I rely on. Thus, even those feminists who could make 'inadvertent alliances' with sex workers do not share their world and the oppression they suffer. This chasm which separates us, the fragility of empathy — I as a translator have been only too aware of these. I do hope this risk has paid off, at least minimally.

J. Devika

CHAPTER ONE

My very first recollection: I must have been two-and-a-half or three. Etched in my memory is the picture of Father's mother coming up close, on all fours, crawling, because she couldn't walk. My little brother bawled at her approach; she was brimming over with affection, trying to sing a lullaby. She was ninety. I was also scared. But she was afterall our granny, said Father. That comforted me. My fear finally faded when I was four or five. The scene is imprinted in my mind: Father's mother, on all fours, trying to cuddle a screaming infant.

School

Chettan[1] returned from his first day at school and started writing on his brand-new slate. I wanted that slate *at once*. I was four years old, my brother was six. I howled as loudly as I could for the slate, but it remained beyond my reach. I managed to create a terrible racket; I snatched the slate and threw it on the floor. And earned a grand spanking from Father.

I made such a nuisance of myself that to get rid of me, my parents had me admitted to school along with my brother. On

---

[1] Elder brother

my first day, he dropped me at my class and went off to his. I didn't sit there. There was a pillar near the iron gates; I went and stood behind it. The teacher came to class and saw that I was missing. Brother was asked; he said that he had taken me to class. A missing child! The teacher became nervous. I was standing close to the wall and getting wet in the rain. At last, the teacher found me and carried me back to class. That made me lose the fear I'd first felt about school. The teacher was wearing a white sari. She made sure that I didn't get irritated in class. Good girl, she'd say, if I managed to write correctly. The joy I used to feel then is beyond expression.

My studies ended when I was nine. I had got through the third standard. The school I went to had classes only up to the fourth grade, and I was supposed to study till then.

Valyamma — that's my father's older brother's wife — was the person who took all the important decisions. That applied to me too. She said: 'This girl has finished the third class, she needn't go anymore.' I don't remember the reason. Father said, 'Let her go for another year; she's only nine.' Valyamma was insistent: 'This will do, she has learned enough to keep paddy-accounts.' Girls needed to know just enough to keep track of how much paddy was sown and harvested, she felt. Father tried to argue further, but the truth was that he had no sense of responsibility. It was Mother who had sent me to school. Since my aunt was being so adamant, Father told me that my books would not be bought that year. I wanted to study, but wasn't brave enough to tell Father so. And none of Mother's decisions held any weight at home.

So, out of school now, whenever I was on my way to the shop, I would clamber on the big embankment and skip along, quite merry and laughing, carrying a bag, until I was past the *pappadam*-makers' house. But when the school emerged in sight, I'd break down. I would howl and bawl and make a big commotion. Not able to express the pain of not being able to go to school, I would put both my hands on my head and howl. People would gather and ask with concern whether I had lost my money or something. No, I'd say between fresh floods of tears, I haven't lost any money; it's just that I feel terrible about not going to school. They would try to console me. You are a big girl now, too old for school, and that's why your father isn't sending you there, they would say. I would keep on repeating that I wanted to study, that I wanted to read English. And then after a while I'd stop crying, go to the shop, buy whatever I needed and go back home. This would happen all over again the next day. I found the wayfarers' attention very comforting! Whenever I went to the shop, I would cry on the way.

When this became a habit, it turned into a public nuisance. People stopped paying attention. When no one looked at me, I would stop weeping, dry my tears on my skirt and start walking. A huge sense of loss rises up in my mind when I remember how I used to walk away; there's still a painful throbbing. And yet, thinking of all that crying, the drama, the initial commotion and later, the sense of neglect, I can't help laughing.

Home

At that time, ours was a good house, a big house, with three bedrooms, two hallways and a kitchen. It had a tiled roof. So I always thought of myself as someone from a 'proper house'.

The house had open verandas on all three sides, with seating arrangements built into the outer wall. A water-jug would always be placed near the veranda. Anyone coming into the house had to first wash their feet before stepping on the cement floor. The house opened into a long hall. The first room across was Father's. My brother's room came next. And after that, a room where only we women slept. Then there was a storeroom and a kitchen. In front of our room and the store, there was another hall. The kitchen was very large — it was as big as the rest of the house.

Houses as big as ours were few in that locality. To the right, there was a Dalit settlement. In the middle of it, a person called Velayudhan owned a big house.

Because I came from such a house, I was pointed out when I worked later in the clay mine. 'The girl from the big house,' they'd say. When I heard that first I thought they meant architecturally large. But thinking of it later, I realised that they thought I was from a well-known and respected family.

My father had built that house. He was among the soldiers who were disbanded just before India became independent. The house was built with the money he was given when he left the army. With all that cash, Father thought that he had become a rich man.

As long as Mother had a job in the thread mill, there was enough money in the house. Those days a supervisor in a thread mill earned the best salary. She was dismissed on the pretext that Father had become active in the Communist Party. My Valyacchan's (father's older brother's) son also lost his job for the same reason.

In the family, we were almost like dependents. Though it was Father who built the house, we were always under the thumb of Valyacchan and others. Even to buy rice and the weekly groceries, it was Valyamma who would draw up a list.

Father, for all his bravado, was quite meek at home. When Valyacchan was ill, Father took care of both families. He and Valyamma used to decide everything together. That's how Valyamma gradually got the upper hand at home. Mother was always given a lesser place. The picture that comes back to me is of Valyamma giving the orders and Father meekly obeying them.

Need entered our house out of the blue. While she earned a salary, Mother would come home with rice and provisions. When she lost her job, she couldn't contribute. Valyamma gave us money for expenses for some time. After that, one of Mother's sisters helped us for a short while.

Both of them began to interfere in all our affairs. My mother's sister began to tell me what clothes to wear, and where to go. It was this experience that made me realise that to be one's own boss, one had to work. No one had been able to bully us when Mother was working.

On many nights, Mother withdrew; she would sit by

herself and weep. Soon, even food was scarce. When she was earning, we used to eat parboiled rice at home. She lost her job, and Valyamma changed that. Now we ate only ration rice. The job of removing paddy and little stones from the raw rice was mine; I felt I was worst-affected by this change!

Father had returned from the army with an injury sustained during a football match. He had a small pension. Not a pie of it was offered towards expenses at home. His usual practice was to go off to the bustling wayside in the evenings. There he would eat whatever he wanted. Though he'd buy many kinds of fruit and bring it back home, it was sheer luck if we managed to taste even a morsel! On the day he received his pension, Father would buy oranges and give us one each. This is the only pleasant memory I have of my Father — the once-a-month, whole orange.

Often, Father's room would be redolent with the aroma of good food. We never got anything. When he wasn't buying from the shops, Father would go to Valyamma's house and eat good food. He was received well there, as if he were a guest.

We used to be really happy if Father wasn't at home; we couldn't wait till he went off somewhere or the other. It was then that my older and younger brothers and I played tag and climbed the mango tree. We were very happy when Father was hospitalised for quite a few days because of asthma.

Our yard was twenty-eight cents in area. The three of us learned to play only those games that would suit that confined space: running inside the house, climbing the tree. Once I

grew as tall as my brothers, I played the games that boys
played: marbles, throwing-the-cashew nut, *kuttiyum kolum*

Father would not permit me to mingle with girls. Our
neighbours were Dalits and Christians. Father's official line
was that religion and caste were unnecessary, he was not just
a Communist but also a follower of Sree Narayana Guru.[2]
Yet, he would not allow us to mingle with people of other
castes.

The three sides of our yard were somewhat elevated. Our
Valyamma would make her appearance, as if on a stage,
and shout in commanding tones: 'Kalyani!' Mother would
come out meekly, scared. Then would follow a barrage of
accusations: 'Haven't you bathed the children? Haven't you
cooked the rice? How dare you say that the rice I gave was
full of paddy and stones?' Mother's complaints would have
got to her through the thoughtless declarations made by
myself or Chettan.

Valyamma looked very dignified. Clad in a blouse, a *ravukka*,
she would be smartly covered with a thin towel — a sexy figure
wrapped in a single dhoti with her ample midriff peeking
through. Mother was a scared and trembling figure covered in
a single dhoti and a *ravukka* that was too big for her. I saw my
mother choke in this house; and this made me realise that pride
and dignity come only out of having money.

---

2   One of the best-known social reformers in early modern Kerala, Sree
Narayana was a powerful force in breaking down traditional forms of
caste restrictions in the state. He was associated with the highly successful
community reform movement of the Ezhavas, who were untouchables in the
traditional hierarchy of caste.

Valyamma never took the money that Mother earned. However, she would decide how it was to be spent. She was financially very secure. This is the story I have heard about that security. Our family property consisted of land allotted for farming. When Father was in the army, Valyacchan sold it and cleared forest land to raise tapioca and other crops — this was a large operation, and he employed about twenty regular workers. Along with this, he raised cows on the farm. All this meant a secure income. His children also earned. One of them was employed as a car driver. Another had his own cycle shop. These two and their wives were also ruled by Valyamma. Valyacchan used to entrust her with selling the tapioca and other crops. She was, therefore, a supreme commander of sorts.

I have another pleasant memory of Father — his ability to speak up fearlessly. When people said that I was indeed my father's daughter, I used to take it as a great compliment. He wasn't very busy as a political activist. There was a reason why he acquired the name of a Party man (*partykkaran*). Around the time the Communist Party was formed, Congressmen tried to suppress it. For Party people who went underground, our house was an ideal hiding place. The river bordered one side, the fields and the forests were on the other. You could easily hide, or escape, if the police came. One could jump into the river or hide in the pond. Many leaders had done so. Local people used to think that entering a military man's house meant facing his bullets. And Father did really possess a gun.

When Mother's job was jeopardised because of Father's political activity, she did not have the confidence to stand up for her rights. She believed that supporting her six children and apathetic husband was her responsibility. At this stage, I took a decision. I asked a girl I knew who went to work whether I could go with her. She said there was a job in the tile factory where she worked. The work sounded easy to me when she described it: I would have to pick up pieces of tile, put them into a basket and carry it on my head. I thought that a basket would be light, like a flower! I thought people would dismiss me as a child if I wore a skirt; instead, I went to work in a *lungi*,[3] all tightly wound around me.

In the Clay Mine

My home was in a village where there was no electricity. There were two roads leading to my home. One was fairly wide, big enough for cars and other vehicles. The other was a lane that turned and twisted. I usually took that sandy lane.

The main landmark on it was a thirteen-acre plot known as 'Pattarukayyala'. As you walked on, there was a pond. If you walked right next to the pond, you'd come to the embankment, known as the 'big embankment' locally. There was a single-log bridge there, fashioned from an areca nut tree. Some distance away from the bridge, there was another canal. You'd come to the river only if you crossed that canal. That walk was so much fun.

---

[3] A long piece of cloth usually wrapped tightly around the waist and left to fall to the feet, like a dhoti.

As I was just nine when I started going to work, I had none of the heavy responsibilities that worker women usually carry. My walk to work was always full of gay chatter with the flowers, the grass, and the birds. No worry clouded my mind — the fear of being thrown out of work or being late never haunted me. I would stay on to gaze at the pond, the canal, the fish; I would watch for long the surging of the current through the canal and walk at an easy pace. Well, one wrong step, and I'd have fallen right into the gaping holes left by the sand miners.

Working hours were from six to six. I'd be in trouble if I didn't collect the wages and hurry back home. I had to turn where the big embankment ended. The way after that point was through a coconut garden on the river bank. The men who hung around there playing cards sometimes harassed girls. 'Harass' is not a euphemism for having sex. It meant satiating their gluttonous craving by pawing and fondling us. To avoid this, it was necessary to have company, or run like the wind. If I had a friend with me, I would walk along gaily, chattering, exchanging stories. Without company, the usual practice was to walk leisurely till the bridge and then run for it. I had to run right up to the canal lined by the *kaitha* bushes and through the lane in between. There were more people around here. But from there I had to run again, right through the coconut garden. Pattarukayyala was a big square-shaped plot. The running would continue when I neared that place. Reaching home after all that running, it was as if I had triumphed over something. There was tension in that flight; and also a strange thrill. As if each day some victory was renewed in life; as if it were an achievement, valiant and glorious.

The fields of those days, the embankment, the canal, the river and that coconut grove! Today, I would have appreciated their beauty better. That teenaged girl fleeing from minor threats wasn't able to appreciate the charms of nature.

When I first went to work, many were surprised to find a plump kid like me there. I had a lot of support: 'Uncle will lift the basket onto your head', 'Sister will pick it up for you'. In the evening, I was the last to get out after work. I got one-and-a-half rupees. When everyone bought rice and provisions, I bought some too. I tucked the rice, chillies and coriander into my towel and stepped into the house like a very important person, only to find Mother in anguished tears. Her hope was that I would become someone big through studies. In my mind, I was already a big person. Mother thought that I'd made a huge sacrifice. She would weep, seeing my hands scarred and cut from picking up the broken tiles. Don't go to work tomorrow, she would say. But when I went to work the next day, she held her silence.

No one thought of it as child labour in those days. The neighbours would ask Mother, 'Though it is her you coddled quite a bit, isn't it true that she's the one who's proving useful?' When I heard that, in spite of all the burning in my hands, I'd still feel I was the boss. After working like this for a while, I heard from many that this work didn't bring much money and that the pay was better in a clay mine.

I was quite scared in the beginning. In the end, I went to the clay mine (from where the tile factories obtained their clay).

Though I was quite strong, I wasn't tall enough. 'Hey man, here's a little bird. She can carry the load but can't unload it into the lorry,' said some. 'Load'? 'Unload'? What on earth was all that? They spoke in an unfamiliar dialect.

Most were reluctant to fill up a little child's basket, and many said in a rush of sentiment, 'I just can't fill up a basket and put it on a small kid's head.' Much time passed like this, and I felt like going back to the tile factory. But the pay there was a pittance. A couple of years went by in this fashion.

Then I was told that working in homes was a good way to put on some weight; the food and pay were good, it seemed. From then, I set my mind on finding such work. I didn't know any kitchen work. A girl friend suggested that I become an ayah. 'You'll grow big soon,' she said, 'and then you can come with us to the clay mine.' I felt that wasn't a bad deal. I'd be able to eat plenty of food!

Ittamash

I told Mother of my plans. Working in a house would make me grow up; I would become plump. Mother resisted the idea at first; but then told a distant relative to find me a place in a home. So he went searching, and found me one. The house of a certain Balettan. They asked, can you do any housework? I told them the truth. Nothing except boiling rice. The next question was whether I could look after children. I'll try, I said.

Balettan was a lawyer. He had his own car. He lived in his wife's house. Once a week, he'd go to his own family. And so I worked there happily, with all the trips in between.

Once, during the Ekadasi festival at the Guruvayur temple or something, Balettan and Kanta *chechi*[4] took us home.

Balettan's sister's husband, called Ittamash,[5] was also there. Balettan was one of the ten children — five men and five women — of that family. I was never regarded as a servant. Those days, servant girls were never kept apart. I was playing with the kids and having a good time with them when I saw Ittamash.

Chettan was a student at Ittamash's school. He used to come home and tell us that they were being taught by Ittamash and Vailoppilly sir. I had heard my brother wax eloquent about how Vailoppilly sir used to write poetry.[6] Ittamash was also in that group. And so seeing Ittamash suddenly before my eyes, I was filled with wonder and respect. That day, the house was full of people; one can well imagine the festive atmosphere in a land-owning family with ten children. Ittamash had come with his two sons and two daughters. One son was just my age, thirteen. Ittamash's son came downstairs to tell me that his father wanted a glass of water. I was so happy that my brother's teacher had summoned me upstairs. I went and got a glass of water.

The grandmother in that house asked, 'Where are you going, girl?'

---

[4] 'Ettan' and 'chechi' are suffixes to names to indicate brotherly and sisterly relationships.

[5] 'Mash' or 'sir' are usually suffixes to the name of a teacher, the former being the corruption of the English word 'master'.

[6] The reference is to one of Malayalam's finest modern poets, Vailoppilly Sreedhara Menon.

'*Mash* asked me to get him a glass of water.'

'Well, be back quickly.'

I thought she was concerned because I was going alone. So I picked up Balettan's older child, and went up with the water for Ittamash. He behaved as though it was a scene from a movie; placing the glass on a table, he said I should wait till he returned it to me. Suddenly he crept up from behind me, and hugged me tightly — along with the poor baby I was holding. I could smell danger. Something was about to happen. I said, 'Let go of me, *Mash*, let go.' He would not. He tried to put his hand inside my blouse. I didn't like that. I freed myself by force, and went downstairs. What the hell was this man trying to do to me? I thought he was going to murder me or something. The little child was crying aloud, scared at being squeezed so tightly. Kanta *chechi* asked me, 'What happened? Which room did you go into?' I think Kanta *chechi* knew about Ittamash. 'To *Mash's* room.' I said. The adults said in chorus, 'Why did you go to *Mash's* room? Would anyone go there but you?' I didn't understand a thing. Now I know that if the circumstances had been different, he would have harassed me.

After being pawed by Ittamash, a mere visitor to that house, I began to fear the others there — Balettan and the older boys, like Asokan and Mohanan. I decided not to continue with housework. I spoke first to Kanta *chechi's* mother, Sarada *chechi*, and told her why. She spoke to Kanta *chechi*, and that became an open matter. The servants got to know; people began to talk. 'The girl Ittamash grabbed.'

Everyone said that it was a terrible mistake to have gone alone into Ittamash's room. All of a sudden, I was at fault. I myself began to feel that I had done something wrong.

I felt that I'd grown big enough to work in the clay mine. The scene was just the same there. The shoving and the thrusting — and those who allowed all this got better pay. I worked in Konettan's clay mine first. This was not a child's game. We had to work in the burning sun, full time, not like other sorts of work, where you could sit down for a moment and catch your breath. We'd get only three-and-a-half rupees there, but it was more than other sorts of work, for which women were paid just two-and-a-half rupees a day. Konettan's looks and bearing were like the Malayalam film actor Kottarakkara Sreedharan Nair. He was in love with all the women who went there. I felt that it wasn't good to remain with this chap and I wanted better money, so I shifted to Bhaskarettan's mine.

With that shift, I grew up as a person; I became very bold, quite ready for anything. 'Twirl them around, get your job done, get good wages. But keep your position without giving in to them,' I thought. Each step I took afterwards was in tune with this philosophy.

'She's from a Big House'

The people who worked at the clay mine were either Dalits, and poor Ezhavas like me, or Christians. Nairs and Nambutiris did not do this work. I had worked there for a couple of years before a girl from a Nair family joined for work. Kunhikkavu, that was her name. She became a bigger heroine than me. I was quite fond of Kunhikkavu, but deep inside, I was jealous of her.

If you were seen as a heroine, you got some concessions. You got the lighter basket. You also got tea first — tea used to be served in rounds as the day's work progressed. Until she came, my friends and I used to get our tea before everyone else. This changed, and so did some other daily practices. Don't touch the pitcher with your lips while drinking water, they'd say, Kunhikkavu has to drink from the same vessel!

But more than caste, the root of my envy towards her was that she was a rival. Kunhikkavu was on my side. She knew well that this would make her position stronger. I, however, just couldn't handle the frustration of having lost my pre-eminence! It was quite vexing to hear others whisper in reverent tones when she came: 'Here comes Kunhikkavu.' When they suggested that the lightest basket be kept aside for her, it annoyed me no end. It was she who would bring the drinking water. That was a privilege. On special days, and on days when more loads of clay were sent, we used to order food from the hotel. On such occasions, we ate only after she had taken whatever pleased her.

Until then, it was I who had enjoyed all these privileges. 'Here comes Nalini,' my co-workers would say, 'keep aside the lighter basket for her.' If someone protested, others would explain: 'She's not like us; she's from a big house.' Or they'd say, 'The supervisor likes her — *mestrikku ishtamaanu*.' Or, 'The boss likes her — *mutalalikku ishtamaanu*.'

In those days, *ishtam* meant respect and affection.[7] Besides, the boss Bhaskarettan was my aunt's son. Being a relative of the boss gave me even more importance. Thus I had an advantage, in many ways. As soon as I appeared they'd say, 'Kunhippavoo, fill up her basket!' A bit like in the movies when the hero appears and there's a flutter. I used to feel all puffed up then. Never felt embarrassed about it. I was a little arrogant, in truth! The supervisors never scolded me. But they too had to gain from all this. By letting me preen, they could make me work more. If you are the heroine, then you can't complain that the work is taxing.

Dakkan Toffees

In Bhaskaran's clay mine, I was such a keen worker at first that I was put to work with someone who was good at filling the baskets — Kunhippavoo. If you went regularly to someone to fill your basket, it was common for your name to get tagged to his — the two of you would be thought of as lovers. The others used to tease me about 'your Kunhippavoo'. Some of these would blossom into real romances; some relationships would end when the quarry was exhausted. When people started noticing our association, Kunhippavoo began to hope he could marry me.

After lunch he would bring me toffees — Dakkan toffees. How tasty! Quite wonderful! Those days they were a big symbol of romance. I didn't know this. I would share those

---

[7]   In Malayalam, 'ishtam' can mean a sexual liking as well — Nalini probably wants to point to the different connotation here.

toffees with the others. Through all the questions about who gave them, where they came from and so on, it was established that a romance was on. I didn't bother to refute that either — I, of course, didn't mind a romance to my credit!

One day, Kunhippavoo proposed. I asked him to meet my father. I had picked this idea up from a few movies I'd seen. My belief was that if someone declares his love on the roadside, then all the girl could do was ask him to take the proposal to her family.

Then Kunhippavoo did not come to work. The next day he was there, quite upset — in a terrible mood. The day before Father had shouted at me, 'So, you could find only a Christian boy to fall in love with?', and had given me a beating. I didn't have the faintest suspicion that Kunhippavoo might have asked for my hand; I thought it was the mischief done by gossip-mongers. Kunhippavoo's friends cursed me, saying that I had let him down. 'You told us to meet your father, and he threw us out when we came to your house.' It was only then the real reason for the other day's beating dawned upon me.

There was boy there called Devassy who used to call me, *'Edatty,'* elder sister. One day, he informed me that Bhaskarettan wanted to meet me. I thought he meant my cousin. Then he said, 'No, it's Ayinikkuzhi Bhaskarettan who wants to meet you' — the first name was the name of his family. He told me where I was to meet him — under the shade of a mango tree in between two clay mines. I went there and waited. He came, but he was very nervous seeing me there. Despite all the bluster, those days, men couldn't imagine a girl going to meet a man. He too had chocolates for me. I gave him my usual reply: meet Father.

When I returned, I distributed the sweets and gave some to Kunhippavoo too. He threw away the chocolate he had brought for me. He stopped talking to me after that. The clay mine was functional for three more months. By the time it was exhausted, our 'romance' had died. Two years later, he took his own life. He was a motherless child; he had faced nothing but neglect at home and outside. Many accused me. But I'm quite sure that I did not deceive him in any way.

My eye was on Bhaskarettan, the son of the owner of the clay mine. He was dark and people would make fun of him for that. He was reluctant to get close to me because he used to feel inferior.

In the middle of all this, I had to tangle with a rough fellow, Paliyekkara Anthony. He used to stand by the wayside and drool over me. Once a friend of his, Babu, came to my family, proposing marriage. Father objected again. After that when we met on the road, he revealed that the proposal had actually been for Anthony, and not for him. Apparently, the agreement had been that Anthony would spend the first night after the wedding with me. He warned me to be careful.

Walking through the fields one day, I found myself right in front of Anthony. I had no doubt that he'd grab me. How was I to wriggle out of this? I happened to see an acquaintance, Chandran, approaching from a distance. I shouted to him, 'Chandretta'. For a second, Anthony's attention was distracted, and I shoved him into the field below and ran for my life.

'Wedding'

I didn't marry because I decided to do so. It happened by chance. I wasn't on good terms with Father then. He would never go to work. However, he tried to control me, tell me how to spend my money, the same way he used to do with Mother. Things began to turn really nasty between us. The fact that I supported my brother's marriage also became a big issue. That alliance had shaken our world. Chettan married a woman three-and-a-half years older than him — the older sister of a friend of mine. I had to face Father's blows for having helped him register the marriage. With these two major rows, I was ordered out of the house.

I had no place to go. It's not easy for an eighteen-year-old girl to find shelter. There were many men who had proposed to me or were in love with me. I tried to contact one of them, Chandran, the son of a military man. He was a sand mine worker. I went to his workplace but he was at home with fever. I was waiting for him at his workplace when I chanced to see Subrahmanyan. Subrahmanyan had once proposed to me and had been upset by my rejection. He was the leader of the local gambling and eve-teasing group. I later came to know that he had actually proposed on Chandrettan's behalf. He was in a different part of the business — he used to mine sand from the river. When I told him of my problems and said that I needed to see Chandrettan, he suggested that I go to his home. He also offered to speak to Chandrettan when he came. We waited till evening; when it was late he said that he couldn't take me home, and that we'd better go to his Ammavan's (maternal uncle's) place. Ammavan, I thought, would be a senior person — that's the image I had. Subrahmanyan was around thirty or thirty-two. So I expected that his uncle would be at least fifty. When we reached his place, I found out that the uncle was the same age as Subrahmanyan. Subrahmanyan was hiding at his uncle's, having eloped with a girl from a well-off family. After my arrival at his uncle's home, gossip started that Subrahmanyan had brought a woman, and had married her. If I tried to correct that impression, I would not be allowed to stay there for the night. I stayed there for a week and the local folk made us husband and wife. We went to his home, and his mother and sister began to regard us as a couple. I had to become his wife that very day. That's how my 'wedding' took place.

I've already mentioned that Subrahmanyan had all sorts of shady dealings. He was into womanising and heavy drinking. He'd go to the sand mines; but his main work was distilling hooch. He would also help to have people beaten up, for a price. Such a paragon of manly virtue — and with a fifty five-year-old lady love, besides! Nevertheless, he would get us everything we needed at home. No one, however, could question any of his dealings. No advice was acceptable. But he was keen to lay down in exact terms what we could and could not do. I suffered unimaginable levels of virulent squabbling in that house at the hands of his mother and sister. The mother-in-law was quick to catch hold of all the words that fell out of his mouth and blow them up into a major fracas. It was living hell. She even broke my head once, having clobbered me with a heavy coconut-scraper. Struggling to hold my ground, fighting inch by inch, I was convinced that life is a great struggle: in order to live, one must fight, fight incessantly.

I used to help him sell arrack. Usually, those who needed the stuff would come home themselves, down it, and then leave. He used to force me to drink, but initially I refused. Then once, not able to bear some major tension, I gulped it down without any water. That became a habit later.

I lived with him for three-and-a-half years. He died of cancer and arrack; unable to bear the pain of the cancer, he mixed poison in his drink and committed suicide.

I had two children with him. The older one, a boy, died when he was seventeen. The younger daughter is doing well. She does not find me acceptable, so I go once in a while just to see her from a distance; otherwise, we have no ties. She doesn't know that it was I who provided for them until she was five. My mother-in-law would come to town in secret and collect the money from me. Since my daughter doesn't know that I looked after her, the image she carries in her mind is that of a mother who abandoned her at the age of two.

CHAPTER TWO

A New Job

I started sex work after my husband's death, when his mother began demanding a really large sum from me daily to support my children. Those days, an ordinary woman worker earned two-and-a-half rupees a day. If the work was arduous, the pay would go up to four-and-a-half rupees. My mother-in-law asked for five rupees everyday.

I discussed this with my friend Kartyayani. My first decision was to send my children to an orphanage. She said that if I put them there, I would lose them forever. Suggesting a way of raising money to support them, she told me about Rosa *chechi* of Thrissur. She apparently had a job there; I could earn money if I joined her. What sort of work, I asked. You'll have to 'go along with' a man, she replied. No one would openly mention sleeping together or sex. I laughed, and asked her why anyone would pay just for my company — that's what I thought she meant. Then she explained. It's moneyed men who come; they need women. If you go along with what they want, you will get paid. The moment she mentioned 'needing women', I understood that this had to do with using the woman the way the husband does. I asked her whether people wouldn't get to know if I did this.

This would be at Thrissur, not in our place, she reminded me — Thrissur was far away from Kalloor, those days. Buses were rare, there was just one in the morning and one in the evening between Thrissur and Kalloor.

No one would know; I thought things would be easy. So I decided to meet this Rosa *chechi* and discuss it with her. I'd do this only if I had her word that the money would be good. The men I knew were like my husband, Subbarettan, or Bhaskarettan. None of them could afford to give fifty rupees. Subbarettan had lots of liaisons. Bhaskarettan used to give paddy. Two measures of grain, a few coconuts; his relationships hinged on those. I was struck with wonder when I tried to imagine a man who could give money. Something earthshaking was about to happen. Someone was going to spend fifty rupees on me!

Rosa *chechi* asked me to meet her by the shade of a mango tree nearby for a detailed discussion. That was where my older brother had a shop, and when he saw us, he rushed at us, threatening to beat us, wielding a big stick. Much later, I discovered that he was Rosa *chechi*'s client. She too had no idea that he was my brother.

The Man in the Gold-bordered Dhoti

Rosa *chechi* told me that we were to go to a place where a police officer was entertaining people. I went along with her. We first went to the Ramdas theatre and watched a movie. As we left the theatre, a police jeep picked us up and took us to Ramanilayam.

At that time, Ramanilayam was a theatre too. Everything there was new to me. It was a completely new atmosphere, one I'd never imagined: a full-length mirror where I could look at myself as I dressed, a bathroom in place of the river or pond I was accustomed to bathing in. In those days, my hair was long and abundant. I was standing, relaxed, hair flowing loose, when he came in. A man in a gold-bordered dhoti, with a sandal mark on his forehead. I was an Ezhava, and our community respected Nairs and Nambutiris who carried themselves in this manner. Here was a man like that in my *bedroom*! Stunned, I asked, 'Rosa *chechi*, who's this?' 'Oh, the police officer I told you about,' she said.

I felt as though I was in a trance. There was a full bottle of liquor, and I was asked if I would have some. Rosa *chechi* replied in the affirmative for me. He told me to pour out what I needed — he probably thought I'd need only a drop. I poured myself nearly three-fourths of a large glass. He was flustered and repeated, 'Pour some water, pour some water.' I added a little water obediently. The truth was that I was feeling nervous, something like stage-fright. I gulped down the liquor in a single mouthful. He must have been truly amazed. He had a glass with just a little liquor, topped with lots of water.

He looked like an aristocrat, not like a policeman. It was the fellow who had accompanied him, a politician with a huge moustache, who I had thought was a policeman at first sight.

His behaviour towards me that night was very tender. It

lasted just one night. But my memories of him are warmer than my memories of Subbarettan. This was the person I'd dreamt of, the lover who appeared in my fantasies.

The same handsome man handed me over to the police in the morning. Men can be both tender and cruel at the same time. I learned that lesson from my very first client.

At daybreak, the police jeep came again to pick us up. We were dropped at the Mission Quarters near the town. Just as I started walking away, another police jeep halted near me. Two policemen got out and barked rudely: 'Get inside.' This was during the Emergency,[1] when sudden arrests were common. As soon as we got to the police station, the caning started. We were caned on the soles of our feet. In my anger and distress at this treatment, I shouted, 'Police to sleep with by night; police to give a thrashing by day!' In between beatings, the Assistant Station Inspector jeered, 'So what did you think? That if you slept with *saar*[2] at night, he wouldn't tell us?' Everyone, right up to the Circle Inspector, kept referring to me as 'the girl who slept with *saar*'. From this I understood that my dream-man was higher up than all of these officers. Some time later, the Sub-Inspector came in. He was known as 'Lightning Babu'. His favourite hobby was to roam the streets and beat up thugs, like the cop in the Suresh Gopi movies.[3] He was kind to me. He told them to

---

[1] The National Emergency 1974-75, declared by the then Prime Minister of India, Indira Gandhi.
[2] A corruption of the English word 'sir', used to refer to a superior officer.
[3] Popular Malayalam movie star known for his roles as a crusading police officer.

stop beating me. Come with me for the night, and you will be let off, that was his offer. I accepted it and saved my neck.

I have never seen that handsome man since that day. Even today, thinking of this makes me feel heartbroken. How could anyone be so cruel? I've never seen such cruelty in anyone; nor have I experienced such tenderness.

Accidents

After my initiation at Ramanilayam, I was caught by the police once again three months later. The Emergency was still in force and I was arrested without any reason. A policeman called Gopalakrishnan came for me; all I was told was that the Inspector wanted to see me. I was asked where I hung around during the day. There's a mosque near Kaloor, near that, I said. Okay, be there at night, he said. I thought this was to pick me up. My tactic those days was to keep the policemen in good humour by entertaining them as clients. I waited till nine-thirty. But they didn't show up. The locals kept asking me why I was standing there. I told them that a police officer had asked me to wait there. People were shit scared of the police.

While I was waiting there, two men came that way. They looked like the sort who made hooch. They were talking loudly about distilling arrack. Seeing them come up, I scurried into the teashop right opposite the road and went out through the back door. It was a place I used to frequent during the day. But I didn't know what the backyard was like. I stepped out into the dark and felt wet earth under my foot. I thought it was wet mud and tried to step away, but fell straight into a well.

I'm done for, I thought first, sinking. I came up and began to go down again. The second time, however, I grabbed the clumps of grass growing on the sides of the well. I hung on to that and screamed as loudly as I could, but no one heard. It was a village; no one went out after eight at night. I simply couldn't recall anybody's name either. There was a Christian house next door; I tried to call the lady there as loudly as I could. She didn't hear. I lay like that for some time, unconscious from fear and the cold. The company siren rings at a quarter past eleven. I came back to my senses on hearing that sound and screamed again. A few people collected there. The police patrol on duty also arrived there. They helped me up a ladder.

It was a funny situation. Both the Circle Inspector and the police driver with him were my clients. You should've seen the jam they were in. I was taken to a private hospital nearby. They had to heat up my body with electric blankets. Then I was taken to the police station.

Both these men were helpless. They couldn't come to my aid. There were other policemen as well. Usually when one is taken in a police vehicle, it's the driver who says, *saar*, this woman's been seen here, there. Here the driver was totally silent. In the end, my brother — or rather, the fellow I'd set up as my brother — was summoned and I was sent out with him.

These two experiences — of falling into a well and of

seeing how people could be helpless to assist someone they felt for — stand entwined in my mind. Their helplessness was quite a sight to see. They'd come every so often to the place where I was seated; then they'd go away. They couldn't even say a word.

There was an auto rickshaw driver near the Thrissur District Hospital who used to regularly take us to work and bring us back. One day, someone picked me up and made me wait in a party office, that of the Marxist party. During the day, we had ridden past the office a few times back and forth in an auto rickshaw. Some of the activists there must have guessed that I was brought for this man. They decided to ruin his reputation. Totally in the dark about these plans, in the evening, we climbed a hill to reach a cottage. It was ten or eleven at night; we were stuck there. The client couldn't join us because he was being watched. But we didn't understand why he wasn't turning up.

As we waited there, all of a sudden, we were surrounded on all four sides by men with torches, like the bandits of Chambal. They caught me and started interrogating me. They wanted to know who my client was. I have no idea, I told them, I was brought here by someone who didn't tell me who the client would be. When they found that I would not talk, they began to pick on the auto rickshaw driver. They bombarded him with threats, asking whether he had not brought me for a certain Rajan. I kept denying this.

In the end, they found a way out: 'You stay back, and we'll let this auto fellow go. We need to know who's going to come to find you.' I agreed. We were between two hillocks, on the bank of a rivulet that ran between them. There were about eight in that gang. They'd made a ring around me. It was .pitch dark, we needed the light of a torch to see each other's faces. I sat down, and slowly concealing myself behind the grass, I began to inch away from the circle. I went quite a distance. There was a shrub there which stood bent in a 'U' shape. That place was full of insects and snakes. I hid inside.

They realised that I'd made my escape only after some time. Immediately, a frantic search began. Some ran to the road. Others flew back to the cottage. Two of them came quite near my hiding place. I think they had seen me slink away. They had kept quiet to let me escape. They secretly took me to the auto.

It was as if an unseen power had saved me. Otherwise I'm sure that once their eagerness to catch Rajan red-handed had dimmed, they would certainly have thought of using me. Their major problem would have been how to decide who'd be first. They were of course respectable men; respectable men who'd come to catch Rajan in the act!

The Company House

After this, I decided to go to Vavannur to get away. I rented a house there along with Rosa *chechi*, Sheela, Kartyayani and others. Rosa *chechi* was our leader, and had all the qualities of a leader. She was backed by some experienced people — Sheela, Kartyayani, me and the others were newcomers.

The 'Company House' at Vavannur was isolated. We didn't have any next door neighbours. A canal ran on one side. There was a mango grove on the other side and then rows and rows of boulders. If I remember right, those were the days before auto rickshaws became common. People used to come in cars. There were brokers in the areas around Kootanad, Pattambi and Mezhatoor. People would approach us through them.

These houses acquired their name from the common practice of putting up a board with the name of some company in front of them; this was just a veil. In many cases it was the large *taravads*[4] that later became 'Company Houses'. In most cases, the aristocratic Nair women managed them.

In the Company Houses, besides the brokers, there were also goondas. There were two with us, Manukka and Kunhappa. Of these two, Kunhappa was really a thug. On the very first day, he and I had a fight. He poked me as I was going upstairs. I slapped him across the face. Rosa *chechi* stepped in to make peace. She insisted that I should be pleasant to him and not make him an enemy. She explained to him that I hadn't hit him deliberately, it was all an accident. The matter was settled there.

Days of Happiness

Manukka was my favourite. Whenever I had trouble, he would be by my side, offering comforting words. He was six

---

[4] Here the reference is to the large houses of joint families, especially Nair families.

feet tall, didn't need sex with women, and was more than happy with touching and fondling. He preferred sex with men. Because he was born to his father's second wife, he had suffered much neglect. He never married. When Kunhappa became involved in a police case and left the place, the love affair with Manukka heated up all the more.

Sometimes we'd feel so fond of each other that we would sit in the family room in the Regal Hotel at Kunnamkulam and talk for a long time. In general, those were happy days that flew by fast. I used to send home money very regularly. Though I was not in a situation where I could go back home, they accepted my earnings. The usual method was to send the money to my husband's mother through a woman friend.

Those days, we had more freedom. There weren't as many social problems or police raids as there are today. Staring and gawking were also not so common. I have vivid, brightly-coloured memories of going out with a client named Siddique. There were five of us: Manukka and Kunhappa as bodyguards, and an admirer, Ismail. Unlike today's gang rapes, this was a real celebration. We would all drink and smoke together. I would have sex with Siddique, and lie beside Manukka.

We couldn't continue this for long. I fell out with Rosa *chechi*. I had had sex with her lover, Abu, with her permission. But the clothes I'd been wearing then were torn. He noticed this, and bought me a skirt the next day. She couldn't bear that. Wild with anger, she opened my box, pulled out all the clothes I had and set fire to the whole lot. Except for the blouse and dhoti I was wearing, everything was destroyed. At that moment, it was a client, Gopalakrishnan, who came to my aid. He went to town and got me new clothes.

In other ways, too, it was getting difficult to continue there. Kunhappa was involved in a murder case, a crime he had committed out of personal animosity. The police had begun to investigate the Company House. So I moved out to a friend's place near Amala Hospital at Thrissur. I made that my base, and continued to visit Company Houses from there.

For some time, my camp was the *taravad* of a Nair woman named Ittiruvamma. A certain Raman Nair kept her company. He was her husband, manager and broker, all in one. This Company House was near Kootanad in Palakkad. Ittiruvamma had a *sambandham* alliance with a Nambutiri.[5] Raman Nair, in reality, was just a manager. Everyone there had triangular romances. All of them knew about them. Therefore, these relationships were quite strong. Manukka was in this house too.

When Siddique went off to the Gulf, the old group broke up completely. I haven't seen Manukka after that. I keep alive the hope that I'll meet him again, someday. Rosa *chechi* used to come to the place where I was staying and create scenes. I have no idea where she is now.

---

5   Literally, 'connection' refers to traditional hypergamous forms of marital alliances, in this case between a Nair woman and a Malayali brahmin man. While these were socially accepted, the children belonged to the mother's line and the father had fewer obligations towards the children than in patrilineal familial arrangements.

I stayed for some time at another Nair *taravad*. Brokers used to bring clients there disguised as prospective buyers of the cows in that house. Our business would be conducted inside, during arguments about the worth of the cows outside. This pretext of selling cows was merely to placate the local folk. The local people knew the truth, but in those days there was a special co-existence among us.

'Maharani'

This was around the time I had started hanging around Thrissur town waiting for clients, after having fallen out with Rosa *chechi*. That wasn't much to my liking. It isn't very pleasant to be wandering around town day and night. For those who stay in the town at night, the main hassle is finding a place to bathe. Using a pond or the river a little away from the town wasn't safe; there was the danger of being attacked by ruffians. The other way out was to use the comfort rooms in town. Not all those who ran such rooms would permit us to use them. The next headache was to find a fairly quiet hotel. Not all such places were safe. Once the problem of finding a regular eating-place was solved, one could while away the day watching movies. After eight, we could seek clients. The duty hours of the policemen change at eight o'clock. Around that hour, harassment from policemen was generally great. If one managed to secure a client, one could spend the night comfortably. If one didn't, getting through the night was a pain. That was really the most difficult time.

Those who waited for clients during the day had other problems. They usually came to town with some excuse — like working in some house or looking after children. They would have to keep a sharp eye on the time. The hassle of standing at pick-up points waiting for clients was bad enough; but even when you secured a client and got your money, the trouble didn't end. You'd have to wait till it was time for you to go back.

One day, disinclined to roam about, I went off to Kozhikode — it was just a casual journey. At Kozhikode, I went to one of the parks and rested in comfort. Then a person approached me and introduced himself: 'I am Rajan. You'll come with me?' He was a well-known broker there. That's why he introduced himself just by name. He thought I had been there before. In those days, one could easily identify a sex worker. Our make-up was a strong give-away. 'Come to Maharani Hotel,' he suggested, 'I'll get you all the money you need.'

Since I wasn't interested in wandering about the whole day, I accompanied him. We took a room in the Maharani Hotel. The room was quite special. You entered a big hall. Adjoining the hall, there was a small door, like a bathroom door. It opened into a small room, with a cot in the middle. There was no light. After sex-work, the person who came wouldn't be able to see anything of us. Once I became a regular there, a man began to approach me steadily. He had something to do with cinema. I couldn't make any sense of what he used to say — very technical things.

He was determined to see my face and stubbornly pressed his point. So Rajan put on the light in the hall outside. The man was astonished when he saw me. He'd thought that we kept the lights off because we were ugly and didn't want to be seen, that people came there hurriedly just for sex. This man wanted to talk to me. He asked, 'You are pretty, why do you sit in the dark?' I told him these were the adjustments we had to make here, and that I didn't know why they were needed. Usually men went off and returned at night, that's all. It wasn't common at all for them to pay us compliments. So I felt a special liking for this man.

That amazed expression which lit up his face on seeing me for the first time remains stamped on my mind even now.

A 'Mental Patient'

I met a man called Salim at the Round in Thrissur. He was in a car, when he saw me standing there, and let me in. He was a stage actor, so he told me, when we got to know each other. Quite well-known in those days, so it seems. He took me to Guruvayur and we checked into a room.

He was terrified that someone would recognise me. So he told me that he'd told several lies while checking in, that I was his wife and was mentally disturbed, that we were there for treatment, that he needed some liquor to sleep after giving me medicine. At Guruvayur, the usual practice is to check in as a married couple, carrying a suitcase. If suspicions are aroused, the room rent zooms up. Some may even leak the news to the police. He had crafted the story of the 'mental patient' to excuse any behaviour on my part that may not have exactly suited a wife's status. He came to meet me many times after this. That relationship continued till I left Thrissur. It began on the road, and ended there.

The Raid and the Sari

Velayudhan, from Palakkad, who I met at Chettiyangadi by chance, became my client. He worked as a salesman for major cloth-mills. He was a very affectionate man; he would put me up in posh hotels and buy me saris.

There's a story behind the saris. Once when I went to Chottanikkara, the famous temple-town, I had carried just one set of clothes. He insisted on going back a second time to the temple. I draped the bed sheet around me, washed all my clothes, and hung them up to dry. Suddenly the police knocked on the door. It was a dangerous moment, I could've been arrested stark naked. I escaped only because Velayudhan rose to the situation. When the police asked him to call me he told them very convincingly that his wife was ill, that she had taken some medicines and was now resting. He was so smart; they swallowed the story of the illness and the mess that could follow if the patient's sleep was disrupted! After that, whenever he came, he always brought me a sari.

Viswanathan's Study Classes

Once, on the suggestion of a client from Thrissur, I went to Kalamassery. I was visiting another friend near the watch company there. I waited near a small shop. People coming there stared, quite interested.

Then someone came up. A somewhat bald person; a huge fellow, quite like a thug, at first sight. He was puffing a cigarette and smiling in a strange way. I didn't think at all that he was an important officer; I thought he was some especially lecherous rich fellow. He asked me who I was waiting for. I told him the name.

He tossed aside a matchstick after lighting his cigarette, and in hushed tones, asked me if I'd 'meet' him instead. I can't ignore folks who have money. There are two reasons for this. One, such people try to behave with dignity (usually, only the effort would be there, there would be no dignity). And besides, they take you to the hotel you suggest, give you money and don't dump you outside in the middle of the night.

I agreed. He wanted to know where we could meet at Thrissur. That confused me, since I usually hung around the KSRTC bus station at night. But if I said that he'd think I was one of the cheap sex workers. That would make me feel a bit small. The better ones all wait in the turning on the way to Ramdas Theatre from Ragam Theatre. Now, to say that I'd wait there would also be unsafe. There were great-looking women there and he'd fall for them. So I told him that I'd meet him at Ramdas some distance away. That was a convenient place as no one would think I was a sex worker; also, there wouldn't be other women out to seduce him.

As for me, I was insistent that I wouldn't wiggle my hips and arms to catch anyone; the client had to come to me.

(Of course, the other thing was that once I stood at a place five times in a row, that became a pick-up point.) I usually recommended two convenient times to meet. Either the time the movie ended or when it started. These were suitable because if it was before the movie, people would think I was waiting for my husband and kids; if it was after, they'd think I was waiting for my family to pick me up.

The first occasion, he came right on time. He bought me a glitzy sari and told me to change into it. All this preparation was to make people think I was his wife. The sari matched the colour of the blouse well — those days I didn't know how to select saris that matched blouses. After that, he got me a mangalsutra from a shop that sold gold-plated jewellery. Then we went off to Shornur. That was a place where sex workers could get a room quite openly. He didn't pick me up from Ramdas Theatre. I was put on a bus and told to get down before Amala. He then came there on his bike and we set off together for Shornur.

It was his practice to get me a sari and a chain like this every time we met. I was terribly thrilled, not at being in Viswanathan's company, but because of these gifts. He used to spend more on the journey with me and other things than on the chains and saris. But it was a different experience. Waiting for him wasn't so easy. On the first day, he was on time. Later, he used to be late. The shift was delayed, he'd say. Or that he couldn't escape his friends. Sometimes other people would approach me while I was waiting for him. I'd tell them that I was waiting for someone. After some time they'd return, and finding me still there, pick up a quarrel. It was awful tension, that waiting! If he was the first to come, he'd be standing there, leaning on the vehicle, tense, wondering whether I would turn up. I'd arrive, running.

Viswanathan was a strange man. He wasn't too handsome and was past forty. He used to enjoy driving a lot. And me, I was always scared to ride a bike. I'd hang on, hugging him tight. When we fell into a gutter, I'd hold him tighter still. He used to get a thrill from that. Those rides are still green in my memory. It was only when I saw the hero flying off on his bike with a scared creature clutching him in Bhagyaraj's film *Chinnaveedu* that I understood what it was all about!

Viswanathan was an important officer in a watch factory. He had a family — wife and kids. Judging from the way he threw around money, he must have been very secure, money-wise. Those days, clients used to be very much like husbands. We couldn't ask them anything about themselves, but they wanted to know every single thing about us. And even when they deigned to tell us something about themselves, it would be with a holier-than-thou attitude.

Viswanathan would take me to fairly good hotels, but otherwise it was like being in school. Tuck the sari pallu in like that, he'd suggest; don't wipe your face on the sari; don't stare at anyone while eating, don't do this, don't do that. That put me off; it was suffocating. I would be dying to know the gossip, to find out who was sitting opposite us, and whether the one with him was really his wife or not. And whether the girls making the big money were glamorous.

Once, in the Elite Hotel at Guruvayur, I was sitting hunched in my chair, when he said: 'Don't sit like that, sit up straight. Place your arm like this.' But all that slipped out of my mind. He was making a note of everything. I crossed my hands tightly when I felt I wasn't being stylish enough. And I looked straight at him and at the manager who was observing all this. The more he tried to force me to behave in a certain way, the more I'd make things worse.

The directions continued even in bed: don't snore, people who snore aren't good, so be careful. And then when he fell asleep, he'd emit gargantuan snores, which could well compete with the Pandava Bheema's fearsome battle-cries. He'd ask me whether he snored in his sleep, and I'd demurely reply that he didn't snore at all. His wife had apparently told him, 'Viswettan, you don't snore at all.' She must have been buttering him up. He was always keen to proffer advice about washing my mouth well and brushing before bed. However, the crumbs from his meals would inevitably be discernible on some corner of his face.

Since we went there together, the staff at the lodge used to think that we were a married couple. He would bring liquor every time, a half-bottle. That was equal to only a drop, for me. He always poured out very little. Those days, I didn't know about small and large pegs. My measure was pretty simple: take the bottle, pour out what you need. Since I was familiar with his ways, I fortified myself before I came. He'd pour me a bit and then cap the bottle. When he moved away, I'd pour myself what I needed. He'd be amazed to see me get so high from what he had poured. He'd get high after some time. But I'd still be in control. And listening to all his foolish talk, I'd be laughing away. 'You're laughing at all this because you are high,' he'd say. I would actually be thinking, 'Oh, what an idiot you are!' He used to be perturbed by the fact that I drank as much as he did. Because I was a woman, he'd pour lots of water into my drink. My habit was to pour less water than liquor. I'd run off to the bathroom in between when his talk got too boring. Anyhow, it was through dealing with him that I learned my table manners.

Viswanathan used to talk a lot. He would go on and on about the faults of employees under him, about the praises showered upon him by his seniors. It was the same story, every time. After a few repetitions it would become awfully boring. But I had to give the impression that I was listening to him keenly. I'd pretend to like all the gabbing: 'Oh, really? It really happened like that?' When things would become really insufferable, he'd ask whether I was sleepy, and then I'd sweetly say, 'No, I'm listening.' Then, at the end of my tether, I'd tell him, 'Viswetta, I'm sleepy.' That would floor him — that mode of address, 'Viswetta'. He really liked that.

In Viswanathan's stories, he was always the hero. He did this, did that, taught his junior officer a lesson, left his senior gaping with admiration, shamed the crafty fruit seller who'd tricked him by taking back the stuff the next morning. That his son waved him bye-bye that morning; his wife had said, 'Be back soon, Viswetta.' He was the shining icon, everywhere.

In between, he'd demand that I say something. I would tell him about my girl friends. How they created a fuss when their clients refused to pay up, and so on. He'd not allow me to finish; he'd interrupt me and say, 'That's all very cheap. Asking for money right at the start will kill the interest in sex.' And he would compliment me on doing the right thing. I'd be bursting with laughter. I didn't take money from him right in the beginning only because I was sure he'd pay up.

When I talked of my friends, he'd inevitably say, 'Not about those dirty women, say something else.'

This would make me angry. I'd retort, 'I went out with a *saar* yesterday.'

There are three types of clients. Those who can be addressed by their names can be considered locals. If referred to as Chettan, you can infer that they are moderately successful. But *saar*, definitely, is high-class. Now, if I address a *saar*, the response would be as if there were only one *saar* in the world — himself: 'Oh, that must be some policeman.'

'No, a big officer, like you.'

That would put him off colour. One day, I told him, 'Viswetta, I had a glamorous client, yesterday.'

'Who was that?'

'A. Gopiettan.'

That name seemed to put him at ease.

'He was really nice. And handsome too.'

'Handsome' made him worried.

'What's the use of their good looks. All their earnings

go to their wives. And anyway, how much does a policeman earn?'

Another day, I presented a story that I'd been going out with another *saar*. (That was a sorehead of a *saar*. I just wanted to make this chap envious.)

'Which *saar*?' he asked, 'Oh, that wouldn't have been a *saar* at all. He's probably doing some other work.'

'No, a glam *saar*,' I insisted. 'A big officer!' That made him pretty moody.

If I told him about others who paid better, he would retort, 'More pay, more work.'

Despite all this, he was harmless. People who talk too much, making a big nuisance, turn out to be all right in bed. Talking gets the 'sex only' attitude out of their minds. Talk too much, and the enthusiasm for sex wanes.

I can't stand people who try to establish their authority over me for very long. One day, I skipped an appointment. That ended the relationship.

At Mangalore

I couldn't stay very long at the friend's house in Thrissur, so I began to work again in Mangalore. The most conducive atmosphere for sex work is to be found in the Company Houses there. I first worked at a Company House that had a Supari label. Once in ten days, I'd move from one Company House to another.

For some time, I stayed in a brahmin household — mother, her son, and his wife. Food and lodging came free there. I'd pay them commission whenever I had a client. I also used to go out for work. Really, I was almost a family member there.

After that, I met someone called Koyakka while staying at the 'Anila Company'. He was then a regular at the 'Reena Company'. (These were the names of the women who ran these places.) Koyakka would come occasionally to us. When we got close, he asked me about myself and got to know the whole story of my life. When Koyakka began to visit us regularly, Reena came there and created a major row. She got hold of my box and gave it away to someone. Everything I owned, including my clothes, was in that box. Koyakka heard about this, came there and got me back my box.

He suggested I shift to another house, and took one on rent. I stayed there and continued my work at the Supari Company. Koyakka would come often. That was a life of freedom, a life without fear.

The *Sayipp's* Ring

Hari was the agent at Mangalore who arranged women for *sayippanmar* — white men. He'd heard of me from Koyakka — that there was this beautiful girl who's this, who's that, all very fancily put. One day Hari told Koyakka that a white man had come, who wanted a second wife, a really beautiful girl. He wanted me to meet this white man. So he came and met me. I spent a night with the *sayipp*. He'd paid me three hundred rupees in advance. The *sayipp* now wanted to marry me. He had some demands. When he came home from the ship, I had to be with him. For that, he'd build me a house and make me comfortable.

I didn't believe any of that. Around midnight, he took off his ring and put it on my finger. It was a hugely expensive ring, set with seven pearls. By the time it was dawn, I started feeling scared. What if he claimed that I had pinched it? I was so scared that in the morning I took off the ring, entrusted it to Hari and told him that I was ready to marry the *sayipp* but didn't want the ring. But Hari didn't return the ring to the *sayipp*. The next day the *sayipp* didn't find the ring on my finger and made a big hue and cry, alleging that I had agreed to marry him so that I could swipe his ring. The truth is that I had returned it. But there was no way I could convince him that I'd given it back. He was so angry; he used me that day, and left without paying.

Even at that time, I was sending money home, though I never saw the kids or my husband's mother. Once, the sum I had sent came back unclaimed. I made enquiries through a friend. Apparently, my husband's younger brother had gone off to work in the Gulf and was sending plenty of money back home. So they had decided not to accept my money. The fear was that if they accepted my money, I might claim my children later. It was painful to cut my ties with them for good; but they were living well, and I found some happiness in that.

I had got into this trade to support my kids. Like any other job, this one too had been tiring at times. I'd carried on only for their sake. Now that responsibility had ended; I began to think of other options, including that of leaving the trade.

CHAPTER THREE

Married, Again

I was confused, unsure of my next step, when Koyakka proposed to me. He promised to marry me and settle down in a house in another part of Mangalore. He had been married twice, he told me, but since there were no kids, he'd divorced both wives. He set a condition for us. If we didn't have children, he'd give up this relationship too. If we did, then we would live together for all time.

I didn't have a bad opinion of him. I decided to accept his proposal, given everything. And so we started living together like a married couple in a rented house at Mangalore.

Koyakka worked in the harbour. He was a loader there: a respectable and strong man. But I soon found out that what he had told me wasn't entirely true. He had told me that he'd left both his wives, but the second wife had gone to have her baby, and had returned after her delivery.

Koyakka's plan was to put us up together. There was no objection to that from the community either. She was a good woman; she used to call me Taatha.[1] But as the days passed, things soured between us. I was denied the status I desired.

---

[1] Sister

I had a strong sense of self-respect; it wouldn't allow me to accept a second-class status. Once her parents came to live with us, the situation worsened.

Haram-haraat?

I was pregnant by then. I suggested that I abort, but Koyakka didn't agree. It became impossible to continue in that house. His sister and her husband had also come to stay with us. They had all heard by then that I had been a sex-worker.

This seemed convenient; his brother-in-law started inviting me to bed. Of course, if the news spread, the fault would all be mine!

Finally, when I was six months pregnant, I rented another house. Zeenat was born there. Until the baby was born, Koyakka used to take care of everything, but after her birth, his interest began to wane. I think there were others influencing him. His argument was that he couldn't accept a child by a woman of a religion different from his own.

I realised his intentions when he made a bad joke once. The child by his other wife, Nusrat Banu, was one-and-a-half years old; Zeenat was just three months. Nusrat was the exact replica of her mother; Zeenat, the very image of her father. When Koyakka was taking Nusrat to show her to his mother, I asked him to take my daughter along too.

He replied, half-jokingly: 'I'll abandon your girl on the train. The kid born *haraat* (in faith) must be cared for, but not the kid born *haraam* (outside the faith).' I didn't know the exact meanings of the two words, but the way he put it really hurt me. With this I decided that she would be raised as a Muslim once I found someone she could call father.

When I found out that Koyakka was thinking of disowning the child, I decided to end that twenty-month old marriage. I was determined to divorce him before he divorced me. Finally, we reached an agreement. After three months, once I found the means to live, I would go back to my place.

After three months, when I was about to leave, he gave me these things: a feeding bottle, a towel and a new dress. Well, I wasn't in a mood to cringe and ask for more.

Back to Thrissur

I had a lover at Mangalore who took care of me when Koyakka began to wriggle out of this relationship: Velayudhan. He had been my client much before Koyakka entered the scene. Both of them worked at the harbour. When he heard that I was going back home, he came to the railway station to tell me that I could stay back in Mangalore if I wished. I was sitting in the train. Hearing that Velayudhan would be coming, Koyakka made this offer, as if it were a big favour: 'Velayudhan and I will support you together. Let's stand together.' He acted as if he'd never seen me before. I was frightfully angry and had worked myself into a rage when Velayudhan arrived. I realised that one fellow had come knowing that the other would turn up.

Koyakka was a very well-built man; he always walked around with his muscles bulging. He wouldn't hurt anyone but would always present himself as a rowdy man. Before him, Velayudhan was only a kid — he stood there scared to death.

'It's nothing, Koyakka,' he murmured, 'I came to see *chechi* since she's leaving.'

'Neither of you should have come. You don't have to bother. I've decided to leave,' I said in anger.

Velayudhan would have liked to invite me to stay on. But he didn't have the guts to do so in front of Koyakka. Besides, he wanted me to be there for both of them. I would never have been able to agree to that. Having sex workers this way was common in Kerala too in those days. One fellow would pose as the husband, and the other as the brother.

Everyone wanted me. Their problem was that I had a baby. Koyakka, who'd once agreed to take care of the baby, was on the verge of saying that the baby could be cared for in an orphanage. Velayudhan would bring me food and clothes when he came to see me, but nothing for the baby. She was born after all when I was with Koyakka, and so she was a Muslim baby. But it seemed all right to accept the Muslim baby's mother! This was how Velayudhan viewed me, with such prejudices. I told them firmly that I was leaving. A man was watching all this – a client who saw a chance brewing here. He followed me into the train. At a station before Kozhikode, he said, 'Let's get down here and stay in a lodge.'

I fixed the rate and then got off the train with him.

He said, 'I am a doctor.'

I replied, 'I've seen many, many doctors, and more important people. I've been around this scene for quite some time. I don't want your status. What I need desperately is money.'

He went out and was back with clothes, many toys and other things, including baby food. He felt I'd hang on if he assumed the role of the child's protector. I stayed with him for a night. At dawn he gave me three hundred rupees. That was a big sum those days. More than we had agreed upon.

I went to Thrissur. Velayudhan came down when he heard of this, planning to stay with me now that Koyakka had lost interest. I booked a room at Dhanya Lodge through him. He would act as my 'husband' while I did sex work. There were problems. To stay on in Thrissur, we had to deal with tough guys. Many places there were ruled by them. The very first week, I locked horns with one of them, a fellow called Wilson. He used to hang around Popular Automobiles, near the KSRTC bus station. His hobby was to lift girls new in the trade and enjoy sex for free. Once he set his mind on a girl, he was sure to have her. One day, the very first week after I'd arrived at Thrissur, I was resting at Dhanya. Suddenly we were warned of a police raid. I ran and hid in the terrace. The police searched the rooms and went away when they couldn't nab anyone.

I was coming down after a while when I found Wilson in front of me. 'Who the hell are you, woman?' he asked. I snapped back in the same tone, 'Who the hell are you, fellow?' 'I'm *Vekili*', he said. He was notorious in those parts as *Vekili* Wilson — Wilson the Wild — and though shuddering inwardly at the sight of that infamous thug, I wasn't ready to give in. I growled, '*Vekili*? What sort of name is that?' The quarrel grew hot. The manager appeared and implored me to keep this guy in good humour. So I bedded a man for free, for the first time after Manukka. With Manukka, there had been love. This was the first time I was giving a thug pleasure for free. After that we became friends. Now he works as a watchman in the town. I see him once in a while. Anyway, Velayudhan and he became competitors. My daughter would call Velayudhan *maama*[2] and Wilson, papa. I had to finally get out of the relationship with Velayudhan. There were problems even then. Wilson had no sense of responsibility. He didn't have the capacity to look after a kid.

Two of my friends, Sheela and Vijaya, were with me during those days. Sheela told me that her friend would care for the baby, and it wouldn't be too expensive. I began to go to work, en-trusting my kid to this woman. After two or three days, I got to know that I'd have to pay her a hundred rupees a day. She was taking care of many kids that way. But that was just not possible for me. I would take her with me for four or five days. Those days, I'd go with clients only after ten o'clock at night. Day and night, we were in the town. If it was the KSRTC bus station one day, it'd be at the railway station the next. I had enough of life as a sex worker. The atmosphere was such that it seemed impossible to go on. My daughter was a year old by then.

The Marriage that Lasted

One day, Sheela and I were roaming in the vicinity of the KSRTC bus station when a fairly good looking man alighted;

---

[2] Maternal uncle

his suitcase seemed to indicate he was Tamil. It was apparent that he was looking for a woman. Sheela said 'It's you he's going to pick up'; 'No,' I said, 'it's you who's going to be chosen.' The lot fell to me. He checked into a first-class lodge.

Right then, he gave me two hundred rupees and asked all about my life, how I happened to have a baby with the Muslim name Zeenat, and other details. Once he had heard everything, he asked, 'Are you interested in living with me?' I was wary, in the light of my earlier experience. But he persisted. He said we could live as husband and wife, that he would bring up Zeenat like his own child. He belonged to Nagercoil in Tamil Nadu and was a businessman. He promised not to tell his relatives that I was a sex worker. He had married once before but his wife had eloped with someone. He had two kids by her. He provided for them. He added that after his wife's elopement, he didn't want an ordinary marriage. Even then I wasn't too keen. There are many clients who make such statements. It's a tactic to extract maximum pleasure and comfort for the moment, and they forget their promises soon. But this man was different. He came again, many times, and tried often to persuade me.

Then, one August 15th, Independence Day — we cannot go to the field on such public holidays, as hooligans throng the place — Sheela suggested that we go to her house. This would be the first time that I would stay at a sex-worker's residence. When we reached there, the situation was pathetic. She had a client; but she also had a liaison going with his younger brother. I was taken there so that she could find a way out of her dilemma. I wasn't ready to tolerate this, and so I cleared out of that place right then.

It had been three days since I had entrusted my baby with the nurse. I didn't have a single paisa. The man turned up that day and raised the issue of marriage again. 'This is my condition,' I told him. 'You don't have to marry me; can you just do me a favour? My baby's been put up at a place. I'm in such a sad plight, I don't have the money to pay the nurse the balance and get her back. I have to find three hundred rupees.' 'Bring your child,' he said, 'it doesn't matter how much money will have to be paid.' I then asked myself whether it wasn't wiser to plunge into another experiment, rather than go on living this life. And so, I began to live with him in a hotel.

He'd told me that his name was Jayaraj, as I'd told him my name, Nalini. But now he told me the truth. His real name was Shahul Hameed. I changed my name to Jameela. He was insistent that his relatives should be convinced that his wife was a Muslim, even if I didn't convert.

Once we started living together, he and my little girl became very close. I didn't do sex work those days. He had a second wife. She got to know about me. I didn't know anything about her. Like any ordinary client, he had told me that he had a wife who was a very bad woman and that she had eloped with someone. The wife didn't care about my being with him. She'd send people to us, thinking that we had a lot of money. If she loved him for money, I thought,

I need not pay any attention to her. I told Shahulkka, 'Let's not stay in the hotel anymore, let's take a house on rent.'

For the next twelve years, I didn't have to struggle to raise my daughter. We lived as husband and wife. When it became impossible to send my daughter to school, he re-connected with the family again. My little girl had grown very close to him. She had begun to call him Papa.

Shahulkka was the eldest in a family of ten. He was respected by everyone in the family. So I too was given a very high status. They were not told anything about me, except that I was a widow. His relatives held me in high regard. I used to be in the lead when there were special occasions in the family, like marriages and other rituals.

Shahulkka's business was making plastic name boards and badges. We couldn't settle down anywhere; we were forever on the move. When there were big orders, we would sub-contract them to other places and keep the supply steady.

My Daughter's Education

It was my little girl's education that was worst affected by this constant shifting. I wasn't able to send her regularly to school. I hired tutors to give her the school lessons she missed. I gave her life lessons myself.

Though she was an only child, my daughter was never very naughty. Her biggest flaw was her habit of responding to any request with the phrase, 'Am I not an only daughter?' 'Am I not an only daughter, why should I be working in the kitchen?'; 'Am I not an only daughter, why should I wash the dishes?' That was her style. She, of course, believed that she was an only child. And she used to claim that she was 'Mama's and Papa's little pet of a daughter'. That was a ruse to wriggle out of work. She wasn't lazy while studying. But when she'd try to slip out using the 'only daughter' excuse, I sometimes resorted to smacking her. That would be usually effective for six months: she would try, for a while, to be a good child.

It was hard for her to understand why some people insulted her. One day, when someone abused her, she came to me and said, 'Amma (Mother), someone called me *mayil*.'[3] I told her, 'Never mind, dear, it's okay to be called a *mayil*, a peacock.' She insisted, 'No, Amma, they didn't mean *mayil*, they meant *mayir*!' She had some innately good qualities. She would never utter obscenities.

Another tendency was to never ask for more when she ate sweetmeats she liked from the neighbours'. Instead, she'd always ask whether they were bought or home-cooked. If the reply was the latter, she'd ask for the recipe so that Mama could make her some. Or if Papa took her shopping, she'd never directly ask for the things she saw there and liked. She'd just say, 'There's this shop, there are pretty bangles there; this shop has nice dresses.' That was her way — just to mention that there was a shop where the stuff she wanted was available. As long as Papa was around, she wouldn't ask me.

She started menstruating at twelve years and eight

---

[3] *Mayil* in Malayalam means a peacock — but *Mayir* (public hair) is an obscenity — it was the latter that was hurled at her.

months. Shahulkka was a good man. He used to think of her as his own daughter. But my mind was preoccupied; I knew of cases where young girls were being sexually harassed by step-fathers. What if for a moment he started thinking that she wasn't after all his own daughter?

When he had an affair with another woman, Shahulkka started playing truant at home. Zeenu began to ask for him all the time. Then I told her, 'There are some things I must tell you. From now, you mustn't sit on Papa's lap anymore.'

I was telling her for the first time that Shahulkka wasn't her father. She burst into tears when I said that. 'You're saying such things because you've fought with him,' she insisted between sobs. I talked to her slowly, at great length and managed to convince her.

There's another thing I've impressed on her repeatedly. It's one thing to love someone. It's yet another to give in just to please him and actually believe that his wishes are more important. We lose our freedom when we submit like that. There are the dangers that may befall us. When she read the romantic novels serialised in weeklies, I would tell her, 'My dear, that's not love you're reading in there; actually, that tells you how not to love.' She used to be very open with me. 'Mama, there's this one-way romance!' she'd say — there was a boy in love with her. When she got a love letter we would read it together.

She knows Tamil, Malayalam, Hindi, a bit of English and the Divahi language. Even though she didn't have much formal education, it hasn't been very inadequate.

Trade at Ooty

I went to Ooty for the first time in 1989. In all towns, there is a demand for making plastic name boards. So we'd move from town to town. This is how we came down from Hosur to Ooty.

The material for our work had to be brought from Coimbatore. When we landed some major jobs to make big boards, we gave up our usual way of travelling with a suitcase and instead stayed on in a room on a daily rental basis. The owner of the lodge took us to be very well-born people and gave us some financial help. With all this, in three years, our enterprise grew big enough to employ eight labourers.

I used to do the work of making plastic name boards all by myself. Readymade letters were fixed on the board using a special gum with acid in it. I knew how to do it if I was given a house name, or the name of an advocate or a doctor, written in clear letters. The plastic is framed by a plate. I knew how to cut that plate perfectly and beautifully. It was a bit like cutting a glass sheet. Besides this, we also used to sell plastic flowers, bangles and women's hair-clips through an agent.

In three years, we made more than a hundred thousand rupees. A good part of that was squandered when Shahulkka started an affair with another woman. Another hundred and fifty thousand rupees went down the drain when the lorry carrying plastic from Goa fell into a ravine after a landslip. All this forced us to shut shop in Ooty.

The lodge owner, who came to know the truth about us, that we had started this liaison across caste barriers, began to feel a great deal of romantic affection for me. What was strange was that his eldest son approved of it. The lodge owner had three sons. My daughter Zeenu was with us and they used to think of her as their own sister. The oldest boy was twenty-two years old. Once the lodge owner told him, right before me, in a mocking tone, 'Hey, lad, you want a sister? Let's do something about it, I'll marry this woman.'

They were Muslims, but he would call his dad, 'Appa'. 'Appa,' he said, 'do marry her. We'll have a sister, then.'

'What's the use of a sister? Won't your Ma come and give me a thrashing?'

Their mother was a quarrelsome woman. She was the grandaughter of some millionaire there. This gentleman had once been very rich, but now he had lost his wealth. Even so, this woman looked down on her husband.

Anyway, the son took this seriously. He was a boy who'd grown up without enough love. Seeing how affectionate I was to Zeenu, Shahulkka and his two brothers, he had set me up in his imagination as the ideal mother. He told his mother's brother that his father had plans to marry me.

His uncle thought it was a joke and humoured him.

'No, uncle,' he insisted. 'Dad will marry her. He told me so.'

'Do you like the idea?'

'Yes.'

He called for me. 'This chap says his father will marry you?'

'That was a joke, *saar*.'

The son spoke again, 'Hey, no, Appa keeps asking, who are you more fond of, your Mama or Zeenat's Mama?'

When I remember the face of that child who accepted me as his mother in his heart, I feel sad, even now. They had all the comforts of life – their own mansion and car. They rented buildings out for an extra income. Yet he thirsted for affection. When they cooked something special in his house, he'd get some of it for us, on the pretext that it was for his friends.

We stayed on the second floor. I never even thought of going downstairs, for three whole years. If I did, I'd go to the bus stand nearby and go to Coimbatore. Other journeys never happened. There was no other romance either. Shahulkka's affair and the landslip together brought that chapter to an end.

'Veerappan's Lion'

In 1992, when we returned to our own place from Ooty, Shahulkka continued the plastic board business. I became rather depressed about suddenly having no money, after having handled quite a bit for some time. We stayed at Beemappalli, which was a centre of cloth trade. I started a new venture there. This was to buy cloth with ready payments and then taking it around for sale. There were two salesgirls too. This would bring in some thousand–thousand five hundred rupees a day. But it lasted only for a year. Until almost the middle of 1993, I lived lavishly — as a proud housewife and trader.

Our landlady there was known to be rough-and-tough.

She used to give out loans for interest. This business forced her to act brash and hard, as if she had a chip on her shoulder. Our house was in the city, surrounded by shops. When I went out with her, people would tease us, saying, 'Veerappan[4] and the lion from his jungle are on the prowl!'

Then I faced a massive collapse. The terrible times started in 1994. I fell ill suddenly, caught completely by surprise. The period stays in my mind like an experience of falling off a cliff, or of being rudely roused from a dream. The descent was as dramatic as the ascent.

On the Streets with My Daughter

The illness upset my life once again. The changes that came were totally unexpected. My drinking habits — of gulping liquor quite undiluted, a habit that had lasted a long time — my disorderly eating habits and my wanderings, all had their effect. It appeared as a swelling in the liver — an oedema. There was a tumour, besides. My right leg became inflamed and broke into an open sore. I became bed-ridden, needing help for everything. Shahulkka was drifting away; he was only an occasional visitor to the house now. Some of his new liaisons grew stronger over that period. Whenever he came, he'd pick a fight. I realized that a marriage of twelve years was coming to an end. He had married me just to settle a score with his first wife who had dumped him. Anyway, I too became pretty determined. I decided to leave him before he

---

[4] A bandit who made the jungles of Karnataka and Tamil Nadu his haunt, and was recently killed by the Special Task Force set up to eliminate him.

left me. I set out, after telling Shahulkka's older brother. He tried to stop me, but I stuck to my decision.

There was another reason why I took that decision so quickly. The differences of opinion in the house were now often escalating into quarrels. Once, when the quarrel became severe, the neighbours interfered. Shahulkka told them that I insisted that he sleep with me everyday, and that the fight was because he had refused to do that. I don't know to this day why he uttered such a lie. Maybe it was the mean shrewdness of a person who wanted to win at any cost. As he had dared to go that far, I too was determined not to yield. I declared that I would never sleep with him again.

Now all my money had been spent on medical treatment. The sore on my leg was bleeding all the more. I was back on the streets with thirteen-year-old Zeenat. Where were we to go? My body would not allow me to do sex work. What was I to do, then?

It was under these circumstances that I went to stay at the mosque at Attingara. That was a trouble-zone. Men would come into the mosque at night looking for women. The impoverished women who came there were tricked into love affairs or kidnapped. The mosque was in an area where people of another community were concentrated. I made friends with some Nadar women to ensure my daughter's safety. There were people who trafficked in young girls. Also, there were many who used them; many who would set up a romance and then betray them; there were inebriated fellows who'd harass us. So at night, we would lay the mat in the middle for Zeenat to lie down, and then we would lie down, making a cordon around her on all four sides. The other three were Nadar women. Molesters would then have to step on our bodies first. That was a terrible phase in my life.

A few rooms had been built adjacent to the mosque, to be used as cooking spaces and rest rooms. There would be no place to sleep at night. Five and six families would crowd into each room. We had to lie down in the middle of the cooking hearth, the pots and pans and other things.

I cannot even think of how I raised my girl during those days. I had to take her along with me even when I went for a bath. When I went to the toilet she had to be entrusted to someone.

Many who were mentally ill were kept in chains there. People like me eked out a living through helping to bathe them and through begging. During feasts, we would get rice. The sore on my leg had got infected. The tumour in my liver was still a problem but that wasn't visible. Since I was a fairly good-looking person, no one would give me alms. To be given alms, you have to create sympathy and that requires high-grade acting.

During this time, Shahulkka came there twice. He gave me two hundred rupees each time. The third time, he brought a friend along. He bought Zeenu a pair of anklets. I was standing in a shop, in the exhibition premises. There was a boy there — Akbar — who held me in high regard, for having converted to Islam. He asked Shahulkka why auntie was living in this place. He said, without the slightest hesitation, with me standing right before him, that I had mental problems. About me, who'd lived with him for twelve full years! At that moment, I decided this man should never come to see me again. Imagine, claiming that I was mad, and then pretending to be my protector! How cruel! With this, we became all the more destitute. Life in the mosque became miserable. There were also other reasons why living there became unbearable: people seen too frequently and people who didn't carry out the wishes of the givers were denied alms.

There was a mahout who used to bring an elephant there who was also a good palmist. He would predict the future reading people's palms and all that he said used to come true. He told me that if I did not leave this place within fifteen days, I would have to face grave dangers. Many warned me that I was better off going away. This man's prophecies never failed, apparently. So I got ready to go, putting together some cash I'd got as alms. Then, unexpectedly, Shahulkka turned up and gave me four hundred rupees. I told him I wanted to go to the Pottalpputhoor mosque but I didn't know how to go there. He took me there. He rented a room for twenty-five rupees a day and we stayed there for six days. Then he went back, promising to return with some money; but he didn't. The second day after he left, the mosque authorities evicted us. There was some space outside shaded by curtains; we moved there.

Zeenu's lack of security became a problem again. Abdul

Razzak was in charge of the small *dargah* next to the mosque. He came to see me one day and asked if he could marry Zeenu. I replied that he could, if he was willing to register the marriage. I was not keen to marry off Zeenu to him. Marrying was usually a trick. What if he had come with a Talaq[5] in his mind? Zeenu was fourteen then. But I felt that we would be safer with him around. He had some influence in the mosque.

While trying to arrive at a decission, we carried on there for three weeks. Towards the end, we had nothing other than rice gruel for food. I felt that it was better for us to go away from this mosque. That day, Shahulkka's sister, brother-in-law, their son, his wife and a neighbour came to see us. His brother-in-law was a *motiyaar*[6] in a mosque. His name was also Shahul Hameed, but he was known as Dorasaivu. He was closest to me among Shahulkka's relatives; this was the husband of his favourite sister. Their son was my favourite nephew. The gift I'd given him on his wedding was a gold ring! He embraced my daughter and wept.

My daughter told him, 'Uncle, we haven't eaten rice for two days.' 'Uncle didn't bring you anything,' said Dorasaivu, and gave her a ten-rupee note. She didn't know that was worth nothing. Seeing this, the neighbour — she was the one who had been with me at the time of my ritual stepping inside the home after the marriage in the mosque — took out another ten rupee note and handed it to her. She used

---

[5] Divorce
[6] A minor functionary in the mosque.

to make a living out of making and selling sweetmeats. She wasn't very well-off. My nephew took out a five rupee note and gave it to my daughter. This was the boy who had been with us for three years when we had the shop at Ooty. I had never given him less than a hundred rupees as pocket money whenever he came. I told my daughter that she shouldn't take those five rupees. 'If you take it,' I said, 'I'll leave you here and go away.' My daughter gave it back. He didn't take it; and so she put it into the collection-box of the mosque.

The people in the mosque enquired about my visitors. I told them that they were was my husband's sister, her husband and my nephew. They said: 'You won't make money to feed yourselves here. Go to Yerwadi mosque. There you'll get food and the girl can find some work.' The worshippers took a collection and the money was given to me. On hearing of the collection, Abdul Razzak turned up. 'Auntie, I'll come with you to Yerwadi,' he said. 'The marriage between me and Zeenat can be conducted there.' I didn't know how to reach Yerwadi mosque; it would be useful to have someone with us. I was sure this man would try to come along on the pretext of the marriage. I let him. When we got there, he wanted to rent a room for the three of us. I said, 'It isn't proper for you to stay in the same room before the marriage. Why don't you do something: get us a room here and you stay in the mosque.' So he got us a room in front of the mosque. After a couple of days, he understood that I had no intention of marrying Zeenu off to him.

Around this time, I met Abdul Nazer. He used to chant

prayers, tie amulets and sacred threads, and look after affairs in the mosque — a *mollakka*.[7] He asked me about my situation, listened and told me, 'Why not let your daughter stay at my house?' Unfortunately, I couldn't stay there as well, as his family would get suspicious, he said.

It was his second or third wife who was with him then. My daughter stayed there for almost two months. In between there was trouble. This man had a friend, who had a son who was mentally disturbed. He suggested that I give Zeenu in marriage to him. I was firm: 'I have no intention of marrying my daughter to someone who's mentally ill. If the problem is that my daughter's staying at *musaliar's*, say that plainly.'

One day, Zeenu told me: 'Mama, you're going to get a love letter soon.'

'Who's going to give me that?' I asked.

She had seen Abdul Nazar and his friend writing a letter together. 'I have made hundreds of thousands by working in the Gulf,' he'd apparently written. 'But my wife doesn't love me. If I accept a woman from the streets, I'll certainly win her love...' This was the general tone of it. Parts of the letters from his wife were also added to it. The letter was thus readied and his friend Nazer came to me and asked: 'Will your illness be cured with sixteen thousand rupees?'

'Who's going to spend that money for me?'

'There's someone. Once you are better, we will find some means of livelihood for you. *Kakka* (Abdul Nazar's friend)

---

[7] A mullah

and I, we are going off to the Gulf. We'll have a grand marriage for your daughter, with ten sovereigns of gold for each of you.'

He was talking of marrying Zeenu to the mentally deranged boy. I saw it wouldn't be possible to go on for very long like this. I sent word for Zeenu, on the excuse that I was ill. They felt they were within their rights to suggest such things, after all, because they were giving her food! But then, because I didn't accept to their suggestion, I also never got the love letter meant for me.

As I was facing this new crisis, my friend came up with a suggestion: 'There's a holy man's (*tangal's*) house nearby, let's go there.' She too had a daughter of Zeenu's age. So both of us went to the holy man's house.

Much later, I learned that this holy man's practice was to let sick people stay there and sexually abuse the young girls who accompanied them. My friend knew about this. The holy man's idea was to grab both the girls. My friend was told that my daughter was the prey. One day, she told me, 'Let's do something, Jameelakka, let's sleep in the mosque at night and the girls can be at the *tangal's* house.'

I didn't realise this was treachery; I thought my daughter would be safe in a place where there were so many women. There was a *dargah* nearby called Hakim Doctor's *dargah*. There was space for women to sleep behind the Yerwadi mosque. We went there.

On the third day, I began to sense danger, a fear that something terrible was about to happen to Zeenu. I woke up with a start at three in the morning from a dream, and hurried back to the house where she was staying.

There were two shelters inside the holy man's yard. One was for the women and children, and the other for him.

At night, he had begun to make strange suggestions and the girls, scared, had crept out through the back and were huddled, terrified, on the side of the rundown shack. 'What's the trouble, dear?' I asked my daughter.

'The holy man came and lay beside Celin *taatha's* daughter. She got scared and called me.'

His second wife and Celin were part of all this. I knew it was too dangerous to continue here. I re-occupied the rented place we had vacated. I had some money, from minor contributions many people had made. And around then, Shahulkka had sent some money with his brother's son.

At the Attingara mosque, there had been more people to help. After being at Yerwadi for three months, I realised that each one there was exploiting the other. My friend thought that her daughter would be saved if she sacrificed my daughter. I couldn't stay there anymore. We returned to the Attingara mosque.

Fifteen days after we reached there, Shahulkka's younger brother passed away. With that, I went back home and stayed there for almost thirteen days. After that I stayed in the houses of his sisters and relations and went to his house only when it was unavoidable. In between this, I happened to meet his aunt, Saboora, who had taught Zeenu Arabic till she was five. 'You don't have to drift about like this,' she said, 'I'll take care of you.' She and her family weren't very well-off either.

Saboora took my daughter home. Her older sister, Arifa took me to her house. For some time, life went on like this. With food, medicines and peace of mind, my health improved somewhat. My strength returned to the extent that I could do some work. I began to take care of our neighbour's child and that way earned a small income. They used to give me food and clothes. But when I began to do housework along with looking after the child, I fell ill again. And that proved too much for them — the food and the medicines. They could not take care of me any more.

Some folk from Kanyakumari town had settled in Thiruvananthapuram. They happened to be distant relatives of Shahulkka. They were associated with the company that makes Horlicks. Zeenat was sent to take care of their child.

Zeenat found it difficult to get along there. As she'd grown up in a pretty decent environment, she was quite skilled in cooking. She was also at ease with all the kitchen gadgets. In their heart of hearts, that family did not like Zeenu's familiarity with a good life. She'd been sent there as Shahulkka's relative. Whatever it was, they didn't like a girl sent there as a servant behaving with such dignity. When she had spent seventy-five days there, I was admitted into the medical college on the advice of an acquaintance.

Zeenu couldn't leave that place now. They sent her to Pathanamtitta to look after their daughter's baby. Zeenu would say, 'Mama, they keep saying, don't talk like this, don't do that. When I say that the dish being cooked will taste better with more spice, she gets angry.'

I would calm her down: 'Dear, you aren't a servant; but you aren't a family member either. You should keep quiet; don't talk of the things you know. That's the law of life.'

In the Medical College

The person who took me to the medical college said, 'There's a doctor here called Akbar. If you tell him that you have no one, he'll take pity on you and help you.'

I was admitted during festival time. I had applied henna to my hands and feet on the insistence of the girls. The doctor suspected that I was actually from some good family. When I told him I had no one, he asked, 'Are you an orphan, completely?'

I said, 'Yes.'

'How can you be an orphan? You have celebrated Ramzan.'

Then I told him: 'I was a Hindu. I accepted the Islamic faith later. That is, I didn't go to Ponnani to convert, so I'm not fully a Muslim. Therefore, I have not been fully accepted as a Muslim. But since I joined Islam, the Hindus have abandoned me. That's how I came to lose everyone.'

At once he called his students and told them, 'Take good care of this woman. Do all that you can to support her — see that she gets food and medicines.'

I got food, medicines and good medical care. Then my daughter came away from Pathanamtitta, not able to carry on there. With her arrival, my situation became tricky. It became clear I'd lied about my orphan status. Although the students were convinced of our helplessness, Akbar Doctor had a competitor there, another doctor who was also a Muslim; I don't remember his name. He went around whispering, 'Nalini isn't an orphan; her daughter's staying with her.' That was to obliquely criticise Akbar Doctor who had given us refuge. The next day, when Akbar Doctor came there by chance, he saw Zeenu. He didn't ask me anything, but he understood what the problem was. That changed his attitude towards me. Then there was a strike, and my name was among those who were discharged first. Not because I'd recovered, but because I'd lied.

Even though I was discharged, I continued to stay in the hospital corridors. When Akbar Doctor got to know the whole truth, he admitted me again. At once, that other doctor ordered them to discharge me. This drama of admitting and discharging continued for twenty-two days. In the meantime, the infection had healed somewhat. I decided to leave the hospital.

I had very little money left, and didn't have a clue about where to take my girl. If I was alone, I could lie down somewhere and die. And she, after having worked in a rich family for some time, was looking good now. All the clothes they had given her were very fashionable ones — very modern. Living with her somewhere could mean big trouble. So we went back to Shahulkka's family home. It was a house on three cents of land, which was occupied by his second sister and her daughter. His father had set it down before his death that anyone in the family could come and stay there. No one there knew that Zeenat was not his daughter. Shahulkka had also never revealed that she wasn't his child. In fact, all of them used to say that she looked like Shahulkka's mother.

Before going there, I went to see Shahulkka's father's sister. She was called Mootumma. Of all the family members, she was the most affectionate. I reached her home on a Monday after getting discharged. After staying there for the night and the next day, I went to Dorasaivu's house on Wednesday. On Thursday, Dora called me and asked, 'Do you have anywhere to go?'

Shahulkka's mother's brother's daughter was staying in a separate house. She was also very fond of me. I had to either go there or stay here. There were inconveniences in the first house — even taking a bath was difficult. But people here were not even willing to let me stay.

'Will Shahul take care of you?' he asked. 'I'm not sure,' I replied. 'There's not the least guarantee that your nephew will care for me.' Then he said, 'Oh then, I will have to dispose off your corpse myself!' This was a man who used to help with bathing and preparing dead bodies before funerals. I first made sense of his statement in that light. But then I remembered, this man helps with male bodies; so he's probably talking of meeting the expenses of my funeral! My marriage had been conducted in that *jama'at*.

So he was worrying that my funeral would also have to be conducted there! Here was I, fully alive. And here they were, worried about the money they'd have to spend on my remains after my death.

I used to be a great favourite of Arifa's fourth daughter, the one called Safi. When my illness worsened, she asked me, 'Auntie, when you die, where will you be buried, in this *jama'at*, or in the Tiruvitamkotta *jama'at*?'

She was just around twenty-eight, and had asked this question quite innocently. But this was clear: people weren't really bothered about helping me in this life. That was one reason I didn't want to stay on in that house.

I was completely exhausted when I got out of the hospital. The medicines had sapped my strength. I couldn't walk easily — I had to stoop and support my stomach where the tumour had been, with both my hands. The medication had to be continued for over thirty-five days.

I would select those relatives who were fond of me and visit them. One day I decided to visit Shahulkka's third sister. I started on my way, with Zeenu, carrying a small bundle between us. I was asked, 'Where are you going?' 'To sister-in-law Hajira's house,' I said. I was immediately handed a fifty-rupee note — a gesture that meant: 'Go away, don't come here again.' I went to Hajira's house on a Thursday. We relaxed there after the evening tea. There was a river nearby; Zeenu washed our soiled clothes there and hung them up to dry. That house had two bedrooms and two hallways, an attached kitchen and store room. We thought we might stay on, until I found a more permanent option. Hajira must have guessed that, and she told me: 'I would have asked you to stay, but there's no room here.'

The kitchen and a hallway in that house were available. I told my girl, 'Pack up our clothes, we are leaving.' They weren't dry, she said. 'That's all right,' I told her, 'they are dry enough. One of Mama's friends lives close by. We'll go there.'

In fact, I did have a friend in the neighbourhood, though my husband's family had once told me I must not eat at her place. I decided to go straight to her house, which they had thought was no good, just to settle the score. Her name was Zulfat. She asked me what the matter was. I told her everything.

'Don't worry,' she reassured me. 'Today is Friday night. You are in my *jama'at* and you are not going anywhere tonight!'

The next morning, the same vague situation continued. All around us were relatives. I had never been left out at weddings or festive occasions. Now that I was down and out, they were enjoying my misery! Anyway, after three meals, I got out of there too. She'd asked me to stay on till Friday was over. Then I was summoned by Pakka Hajira — she was from a big family — no relative of ours, though. She enquired how I was doing. I told her about my hospitalisation. She, her daughter and son gave me twenty-five rupees each.

Our family lived right around the mosque. Doraisaivu lived in the front of the smaller mosque. Hajira's house was to the left of that. A little further ahead, you'd come to Zulfat's house. Pakka Hajira lived next to her. Sister-in-law Havva's house came next. These were all arranged as if on different points on a star-shape. Mootumma's house was located on the fifth point of this star. In my hour of misery, I took rounds of this star like a devotee circling a holy place in worship. All four sides of the star were covered, I thought. That ought to be the end of my problems.

From there, I went to Shahulkka's cousin's house. His wife was a high-born woman. She too was financially shaky, because of her husband's wayward ways, and had lived for some time on alms, like me. I called her sister-in-law Havva. She was quite fond of me. I told her that I was back from a tour of the country. She asked me why I had not stayed on at Kochumaami's place — that's what she used to call Mootumma. I told her, she wanted me to stay on but she was afraid of her daughter-in-law. She reassured me that it wasn't Kaka who kept the house going. No one had the right to order me to leave; I could stay on there.

I asked her, 'How can you take care of me, when you depend on alms yourself?'

'If God is willing, everything will fall in place.'

So I rested there. On the third day, Mootumma passed away. Someone came to invite us to the funeral at twelve o'clock. We reached the house where all the sisters had lived together by late evening. To take part in the funeral meant that you could leave the house only after three days, after having a bath. Now, I was allowed a full bath only once a month; the doctor had allowed me to wash my body only once a week. I told everyone about this. They thought it would be okay — nothing's going to happen if you have a funeral bath! Besides, all the relatives would get together, they reminded me. 'We can talk to Shahul and take a decision about you.'

Though I was married in a mosque, I had never made claims on those grounds to him or his relatives. After all, it wasn't an arranged marriage. It was a relationship that we had jumped into because of a moment's attraction. The fact that he was not the father of my child was also on my mind. So I was determined not to argue for my rights. Everyone said, 'Let's have a mediator.' Shahulkka reached there the third day, making a big noise saying that he hadn't been informed or invited. Actually he had come there to gauge how far the issue had moved, and was fully aware of my presence there.

Everyone said together: 'We didn't know where you were. Your wife didn't tell us.'

I had been in no mood to tell them where he was living with his mistress. If someone went there they could bring her along with him. Anyway, I became the big criminal who hadn't allowed the news of the funeral to be communicated to him. No one seemed concerned about my situation. It all ended in a huge argument. One side was with me and another side, with him.

I said, 'You haven't bothered about how this kid and I have lived all these days. All this big talk about new converts is going on; but no one cared about my girl. So I'm not going to care, whatever you say.'

Then he made a dramatic declaration: 'This woman is after all my wife. I will not forsake her.' If he owned up to forsaking me, he'd have to explain why. Then everyone began to vie for the protector's role. They suggested, 'Sister-in-law, why not stay at the family home?' I said, 'I can only sleep there, how am I going to find food?' Shahulkka had seven sisters. None of them knew that Zeenu wasn't his kid. Then a sister-in-law offered to shelter us for three days until he returned. He gave her some twenty rupees or so for the three days' expenses, promising to return soon. There was no sign of him even after six days. Then Havva's younger sister turned up and promised to take care of us even if Shahulkka abandoned us. I could see that this was a part of yesterday's farce. He had arranged with her to remove us from here. As long as we were here, his good name was at risk.

Then something happened. On the way to the pond where I used to go for a bath from Havva's house, there was a thatched shop near the mosque. The shopkeeper made fun of the way I spoke, as I was from the north. One day he asked me 'Hey you, girl, where is your *putiyappla* (new bridegroom)?'

I said, 'Well, what am I to say, the *putiyappla* doesn't exist, all I have is a *pazhayppla* (old husband), and I haven't the slightest idea where he is.' Pakka Hajira's brother overheard this. He asked me, 'Where is he, has he abandoned you?' I replied, 'He's not gone anywhere. I was just joking when he tried to tease me.' Honestly, I didn't want anyone to know of my plight. That's why I made a joke of it.

He probably guessed how sorrowful I was when I said this. He came to our family house and asked whether Shahul, who had married me in this *jama'at*, had abandoned me. That became an issue in the house. Not the fact that their brother had dumped me, but that I had complained. In this situation, another relative of Shahulkka, Sainaba, appeared and took us to her place. There we found out that a relative of hers needed someone as a companion. This girl was a B.A. student, and she wanted someone from the family to be with her. She assured me that Zeenu would be treated as a member of the family there.

'No,' I said. 'I've had bitter experiences in letting her stay in another place. I'll take care of her by begging for alms.'

However she firmly assured me that Zeenu would be treated properly.

So I let her stay with that family and went to Attingara mosque. I was there for barely a week-and-a-half when they sent word from the house where Zeenu was staying. Sainaba had taken two thousand rupees from them as remuneration for fixing up Zeenu there, and had left. She had been posing as her guardian.

I knew someone called Hydros there. He used to help me — he had one-sided love for me — with occasional gifts of money. I told him about this problem. 'Bring her back,' he said, handing me two thousand rupees. 'We'll find her another place to stay.' I brought her back, and we went to live at Yerwadi again.

Then came the month of Ramzan. During the fast, visitors are few, and that means our incomes also dip. My purse began to get thin. I felt it was time we settled somewhere. I had some money from alms and charity, but that would be over soon.

Sex Worker, Again

Not knowing what to do, I came back to Thiruvananthapuram. The tumour had turned my hair grey. I went to someone to dye it black. I had also decided to get back into sex work. I asked a relative at Thiruvananthapuram whether she could give my girl shelter if I paid her three hundred a month. She refused. 'A young girl. No, it won't work out.'

I then turned to the daughter-in-law there, 'I'll find a small job at Thrissur. Can you do something for Zeenu?'

She said, 'Auntie, I cannot bear to live here. This woman — my mother-in-law — and my three sisters-in-law fight with me all the time.'

I told her, 'If you have the guts, you should move out. Take care of my girl.'

So it was arranged to rent the small house next door. When my husband heard that I was ready to pay six hundred a month, he was ready to play the protector. 'You shouldn't let her stay with a daughter-in-law. I'll put her up with my sisters.'

'All right,' I agreed. 'Do something. Ask your sisters; let's see who agrees.'

He set off at once to ask, but all of them were reluctant. What if she fell in love with one of their sons? What if she eloped? So in the end, he had to return disappointed.

I said, 'This is how it is. Your sisters aren't prepared to look after her. The daughter-in-law is willing. She's not afraid that Zeenu may elope. And if she did elope, she'd think it was a good thing, if it was to get away.'

Once again, I was back in Thrissur. This was in early 1999. I would go twice a week to Thiruvananthapuram to see my girl. I always arrived with money and food from expensive hotels; my girl didn't know what was going on, but deep inside, she was uneasy. Both of them, especially the daughter-in-law, began to get suspicious about my source of income. Zeenat started to probe, 'Where's this from, how did you get this?' I would tell her that I had a man friend who was helping me; that we had to meet the expenses somehow; that Papa had dumped us and so I had to do this.

It was only after the big money came in that I told her about sex work. I could make a thousand rupees a night, I told her; and then I could come back to her sooner. I wanted to go to her as soon as I could as she was living in a very inconvenient place, and I didn't know whether she was comfortable or not. My girl has always had this trait: if she doesn't like something, she'll not say so. Her practice is to keep quiet. She never openly expresses distaste; instead she accepts things as they are. So I still can't say that she has accepted me fully.

CHAPTER FOUR

Trade Union

Having drifted like this from one sort of life to another, sometimes doing sex work, sometimes doing other work, I took a
firm decision to stay on in sex work when I began to interact
with Jwalamukhi, an organisation that worked for the rights of
sex workers. Sarada, Lalita and some other women had formed
an organisation and were working for it. I joined an already-
existing organisation; I didn't enter the scene by creating one.

One day, I had just returned to Thrissur from Thiruvananthapuram, and was standing outside the Municipality Comfort
Station, arguing with the caretaker over small change. Two
women were standing nearby, watching. They came up to me
and hissed, 'The likes of you are never going to get better!' I was
amazed. Why on earth were these people, who I didn't even
know, scolding me?

They actually meant, 'Why are you making a fuss here? Isn't it
better to come to our office?' They told me that the Jwalamukhi
office was at Ancheri, five kilometres from Thrissur. That evening
I got into an auto rickshaw and went to Ancheri. Locating the
place was easy; the name Jwalamukhi had become famous by
then. Those who joined it were known as 'Jwalamukhikal'. That
day I was far too shy to go in.

The next day, although I was still hesitant, I went in. The house was prominently situated, in the middle of Ancheri. A class about 'AIDS' was in progress. I later heard that it was being conducted by Prof. Gokuldas of Guruvayur Srikrishna College. Many sex workers described their experiences. There were free discussions about the way the police interfered in our work and about different types of clients. All this was new to me.

By the time I went there for the second meeting, I was almost, nearly almost, an activist, a part of the organisation. Everyone would speak of her problems; no one seemed to be speaking of solutions. 'On Monday, the police beat me up'; 'on Tuesday, the police punched me'; 'the thug attacked me'; 'I was thrown out of my house'; 'the shopkeeper insulted me.' These were the complaints. No one said anything about how they'd hit back.

I could make no sense of this at all. We were saying that we had an organisation. We were also saying that it had strength. We were going to the police station, meeting people, holding meetings, speaking of our problems. But never did we talk of solutions. I could not understand why. After being a silent listener for some time, when Thresia started to talk, I asked a question. Thresia was a gutsy woman; she could flatten the whole of Thrissur if she wanted to. She could handle any policeman.

My question was whether all we could air were these complaints; whether we hadn't any solutions to offer. Paulson was a bit irritated, and he said, 'She's come to us because she doesn't have a solution, right?' I immediately reminded him that he had told us in the beginning that the organisation had been formed so that we could find a solution. 'If you have an idea, why not tell us?' he replied.

I hadn't the slightest hope that anyone would accept what I said. Everyone was relating tales of harassment and going around in circles. I put forward my suggestion. People had mentioned situations in which one faced police arrest. The story was always the same — the police arrests you, you approach the lawyer, the fine is paid in court; once again, the police arrests you – this is how it was. Many had confessed how much money they had had to pay for a lawyer. This wasn't really necessary at all. Why did one need a lawyer to pay a fine? We hadn't really committed an offence. So we had to fight our case claiming that we shouldn't be punished.

Many were sceptical. 'That's just impossible,' they said. I told them, 'No, you are wrong. If we had two people to offer us bail, we could argue that we had committed no offence. We could argue our case and prove we were right.'

Some of them asked, 'Aren't we in the field to commit offences?' 'That's the hitch,' I told them. 'If you think it's an offence, you're sure to be punished. If you think you have committed a robbery, you'll be first clobbered by the local folk, then by the police, and then the court will punish you. How are we offenders? In what sense? If sex is the offence then there's one more person who must be punished. How come that fellow is never punished? Isn't he an offender too?' Then the question shifted to how a *man* could be caught.

'It's this attitude that prevents us from finding a solution,' I said. 'You think you are in the wrong. The lawyers wheedle money out of you, get you sentences and make you pay fines. They don't care about representing you.'

With this, Paulson, who'd been irritated earlier, became enthusiastic and began encouraging me. He asked me what we could do. That led to a very detailed discussion. The first hurdle was to decide who would offer bail. It would have to be someone with a tax receipt. Many had lovers. Or families. The problem was, who was going to inform the organisation. I said, 'This is what our organisation should mainly do: if you get caught, I must come to your aid. If I'm trapped you must help me out.' Someone asked what one would do if the person bailed out didn't appear regularly. I said, 'We don't have to bail out everyone. Let's do it for those who we can trust. Others may have friends who trust them; let them help.' We then saw the need for a lawyer. Our talk got pretty animated as we discussed who that could be.

In the end, the discussion came back to who was to speak of all this in public — who was to bell the cat? 'We shouldn't stop at meetings behind closed doors, we need public meetings,' I insisted. Before this we had had a couple of public meetings. But not in our own place. I told them I was ready to speak up.

My First Public Speech

The next week, there was a meeting before the Municipal Office. I was given the mike and asked to speak. To tell the truth, it was only then that I understood how tense one becomes when one has to address the public. My hands began to shake with fright. I had no idea what to say. All I knew was that whatever I had to say, I had to say it loud and clear, like the politicians. I picked up the mike and said, 'We are here for the sex workers' organisation. We want our rights to be respected. The police shouldn't beat us. The thugs shouldn't harass us.' When I reached this far, the shivering stopped. I went on. 'We aren't the only people to commit this crime. There are lawyers who come to us; there are doctors and businessmen. It isn't fair that all of them are considered respectable and we alone are made into criminals.'

Hearing my speech, those who were scattered far away came close and formed a crowd. They were all agog, curious to know whose name I would mention first! This was a public meeting without a stage. The crowd was almost touching us. I wasn't sure what to say after that. I put down the mike there, saying, 'If any of you think I'm wrong, please come up and say so.'

Everyone said, 'Nalini, you did well.' That rid me of my fear and shivering and gave me lots of self-confidence. Maitreyan came the next week, having heard of all this. That made me all the more enthusiastic. I'd heard that Maitreyan and Jayashree were active at Thiruvananthapuram; but I didn't know much about them.

In the end, when the march finally began, out of the three hundred to three-hundred-and-fifty sex workers who were with us, only nine took part. Besides us, there was the lawyer Nandini, Maitreyan, two women who had come with him from Thiruvananthapuram, and Paulson. A march with just ten to fourteen people.

Nandini made announcements from a vehicle in front. If a march is to be a march there must be slogans, of course! Everyone was mum. After walking for some time, I raised a slogan, 'Police, be just!' This was a slogan I'd heard in many big, big strikes! I was used to seeing the Marxist party marches.

Molly, who was by my side, began to call out, 'End police hooliganism!' I cautioned her, 'Let's just have, "Police be just!", and not "hooliganism".' But Maitreyan interrupted. 'That's okay,' he said, 'you can say "hooliganism", you don't have anything to fear.' Then we shouted whatever came to our tongues and marched. We went around the Tekkinkadu ground and neared the Collectorate. There the police were waiting with their *lathis*. Maitreyan said that we would raise slogans here once more and then split.

The policemen noticed me. They called Molly aside and asked, 'Who's this?' Though I'd been around the place for some twenty to twenty-six years, the policemen didn't know me too well. The older police fellows knew me; the new chaps simply didn't. Molly said, '*Saar*, this is an old hand.' 'Old hand?' 'Don't you remember giving her two hundred rupees long back?' I had once taken two hundred rupees from a policeman and then disappeared without going out with him. He gave me a sickly smile, stepping away from the picket. That made me bold.

This was in 1999. There was another event towards the

end of that year, a symposium on the topic 'HIV and the Role of Men'. I was asked to speak on 'The Social Position of the Devadasis'. I looked up many books on this topic. In many of the accounts of travellers who'd visited Kerala long ago, there are descriptions of 'Ammachiveedukal' they'd seen here.

I included all this in my paper. My idea was that in a symposium, you talk looking at a paper.

I was to speak first. If this was not the case, I'd just have followed what the first speaker said. After me, Lalita and Sarada were to speak. I spoke of two devadasi families, which existed long ago at Moovattupuzha and Thrissur. In those days, they weren't referred to as devadasis, but as 'Koothicchi' or 'Tevidishi', which of course are favourite words, dirty names hurled at us. This speech was conducted in the hall of a high school. We had a mike. When such choice words as 'Koothicchi' and 'Tevidishi' began to float out of the mike, a crowd gathered quickly. The hall was full.

With this, I abandoned all that was written in the paper. I began to compare these days and those, and talk about today. Today we are called *veshyas* or sex workers. That's quite all right. But ugly names like *petti* and *tatti* must be avoided, that was what I argued. Even if we are not given the status and dignity of the olden days, we shouldn't be insulted and harassed. And so I began to speak, like the politicians do. Sixteen people there had been arrested. I produced figures to show that their clients hadn't been arrested. The symposium began to turn into something else.

But I was conscious of the fact that this was a Partnership

for Social Health (PSH) programme. I reminded my audience that HIV was caused by the neglect of sexual safety measures. Then a Catholic doctor leapt up from among the audience members and argued that the condom should not be used; it was against nature, so he believed. I teased him; 'Pray hard,' I said, 'that all illness as get cured, so you can stop all medical treatment!' With this, the symposium turned into a furious debate. And he was an invited guest. Maitreyan's way was to let it all happen as it did. He never tried to stop us at any point.

After the programme, people gathered around, curious to know about me and how I got into this trade. When I said that I was a sex worker, they said, 'Oh, then Maitreyan must have taught you to speak; Paulson must have coached you well, they are making you say many things.' Even though I had made the speech, people assumed I was repeating the words of Maitreyan or Paulson. I began to insist that Maitreyan and Jayashree were not sex workers, that they were merely members of our support group.

I had another experience while working with Jwalamukhi. There was a day care centre for children there. I met the husband of the woman who was working there as an ayah. I had to stay there for some organisation-related work. On my friend Sujata's suggestion, I went along with this man. We went to a house he had rented at Vallacchira. He went off for a game of cards, telling me that if anyone asked, I was to say that I was his relative.

This was in a spacious building. The room next to the

one where I was staying had been rented out to a sherbet seller. This fellow got suspicious because the doors of my room were often locked. I think bringing women there was quite common. When he looked in I was fast asleep. He stamped hard on the floor to wake me up, and asked me who I was. I told him I was there to take a relative to the hospital. He wouldn't accept this, and said that he knew very well why I was there. 'Oh, really,' I retorted, 'then that makes my job easier!' He thought I'd be scared and submissive. He quarrelled for some time and then went away.

He came back with some women he had collected from around the place. They began to shower abuses at me — it was because of women like me, apparently, that the country was going to the dogs. I wanted to tell them, 'It isn't we who're making a botch of this place; it's the men in your country who're experts at that kind of job!' But it was wiser to keep silent in that situation; so I didn't say anything. They threatened to call the police if I didn't spit out the truth about why I was there. By then I'd noticed that they were not the bravest of people. 'Please do call the police,' I told them.

The police arrived. They saw that it wasn't easy to trap me. You could be trapped only if you looked flustered, or were cowed down. The sub-inspector called me aside and began to question me. 'Why are you here?' 'I came with this man,' I said. 'How long have you known him?' 'Six years.' 'Where did you meet him?' 'At Aluva (I knew he had a footwear shop at Aluva).' 'What's your connection with him?' 'He's a good friend of mine.' 'What sort of a friend?' '*Saar*, whatever your idea of a friend is, that sort of friend.' 'How old is he?' 'Thirty-six.' 'How old are you?' 'Forty-two.' Then he had nothing to ask. He demanded my address, and I gave him the Jwalamukhi address, and Paulson's phone number.

When all the fuss was over, the person who had brought me there showed up again; this was a matter of his pride. He said he wouldn't be able to hold his head up unless I stayed on for another day. I agreed but didn't feel brave enough to sleep there alone, so I got Sarada to keep me company.

You can see all three sides from that house. In the next house, four or five people were standing together, in a group. There were people collected in the house next to that, too. Some twenty people were standing around in various places, all alert, as if on guard. They seemed sure that a gang of thugs was getting ready to storm their houses in revenge for having harassed us. The whole atmosphere was heavy with suspense — as if a bomb attack was expected. The reality, of course, was that two harmless women were staying in the house! In the dark, people talked, moved around, went away.

At eleven at night, we called the police. They knocked at the door and we asked them to come to the window. 'We'll open the door only if we are convinced that this is the police,' we said. The police came to the window. It was the same sub-inspector who had come during the day.

'Have you decided to settle here?'

'Yes.'

'How will you stay?'

'On rent.'

'Have you written out a rent agreement?'

'Yesterday was Saturday, today's Sunday. We're going to get the agreement written tomorrow.'

'The local folk are terrified that you and your gang will attack them at night. What are we to do?'

'No one's going to come here; there's going to be no attack. But if we are attacked, please make sure to note who the attackers are. We won't be alive to report it.'

They were convinced of the real truth then. People think that to win you need a lot of power. No, indeed. If you use logic and have the ability to calculate shrewdly in a situation, it's possible to get yourself out of many a tight spot. I'm very confident of this!

Right in Front of Death

One of my clients in Chavakkadu used to send an auto rickshaw to pick me up. I'd keep the auto moving around until he came out of his house. I was in the auto one day, moving around the vicinity of the railway station at Guruvayur, when we noticed that we were being followed by a motorbike. We tried to dodge it many times, but it was still behind us. We could lose them if we entered the town, but if these fellows raised a hue and cry, we would be arrested by the police and the driver of the auto rickshaw would get a severe beating from the police.

When we saw that it was almost impossible to get away from them, I told the driver to let me out on the road and get away as fast as he could. And so I got out off the auto rickshaw and hailed the bikers, as if I knew nothing. From my own experience I knew that when danger seemed unavoidable, it was best to co-operate with the attackers.

The bikers were surprised at this. Usually the woman gets out of the auto and runs for her life. I knew well that it was useless to run. I would get caught, and get a beating too. 'What's the big idea, woman?' they asked. 'You've been following me for some time,' I replied, 'I thought I'd come along if you are good clients.'

This was new to them. I was put on the bike and taken to Brahmakulam. The bike stopped in front of a ration shop, a half-built, empty building, and I was taken to the upper storey. One fellow used me there. He paid up too. But all the time he tortured me mentally with questions like, 'Can you bring young girls?' 'Can you let me have your daughters?' These were deliberately meant to provoke me, to get me wild. These were fellows who don't stop at using; they must also hurt. It was clear from the questions they asked. They would get us wild, and then beat us. I lied gloriously: 'I have only two boys. I'm quite out of touch with my place.' I held my pace and evaded him. The second fellow came and had his turn. He didn't pay. He too tried his best to get me mad. That didn't work either. Then they took me to a terrace some distance away and told me to wait there, promising to put me in a vehicle at daybreak.

Those who really wanted to set us on our way usually took care to drop us behind the bus stand or the railway station. When these fellows took me to the terrace, I began to smell something fishy. I got down from there and stepped into the next house. There was a dog there, chained. It wasn't easy to see it if you were looking from a distance. The chain was a pretty long one. I crept on top of the coconut fibre-heap in that yard, lay down, and covered myself with coconut leaves. I could see those fellows coming back from under my covering. They couldn't see me. I lay there holding my breath and looking at the road.

A young woman was murdered at the same spot a week later, a girl I knew in Guruvayur, an orphan who was mentally disturbed. She used to roam around aimlessly. When she needed money, she'd do sex work. She was taken to a lonely yard by three men. They were joined by five others. She screamed when she was raped by eight men. They tried to silence her, and she died of suffocation.

I have no doubt that this crime was the handiwork of the same Brahmakulam gang that had taken me there. This murder happened in the same spot, right in the centre of Brahmakulam. All the locals knew who had done it. But they were too intimidated to speak out. We conducted a dharna there in protest. I too spoke at the meeting. It was of no use. The murderers went scot-free. Since it was a sex worker who lost her life, society was not moved at all.

I had another experience of seeing death face to face. I was trapped by an auto rickshaw driver called Chandran who used to drive an auto called 'Pulari' in Guruvayur without realising who he really was. I'd heard from friends that there was a fellow who snared sex workers into places where gangs of ten and twenty would use them. Chandran paid me an advance of five hundred, and came at ten at night, saying that he'd take me to a lodge at Thrissur. The auto stopped at a deserted place between Choondal and Kecheri. The excuse was that it had engine trouble. The engine didn't start even after many attempts. I could see that this was all play-acting.

He suggested that we go into the coconut garden nearby. I could smell danger; I was already thinking of escape. We got into the coconut garden by jumping over a fairly high wall. It was very marshy there; lots of water had collected under the trees. He left telling me that he'd be back soon. I could see no way to escape. Anywhere I hid in that garden, he'd find me. In the end, I dug up the sand in an open area to form a depression, lay down in it and covered myself with the sand. Lying there I counted seventeen men jumping in one after another over the wall. They searched all over the place. One sneeze, and I'd be in their claws. I heard them say that I must have fallen into the mud and died and that my corpse would be floating by morning. They were talking of the trouble there would be if the corpse did indeed surface. They went away after searching for some more time. I lay there till it was light.

I was determined to get even for this. Early morning, I went to the police station and wrote a complaint. Seven of the gang were arrested. Though I was also shut up at the station for a whole day, I savoured the happiness of having got Chandran behind bars.

Ammu

Ammu, who's no more, had a nature quite the opposite of my own. Everything in life was trivial for her. She had written around twenty poems. Her poem about the deity of Guruvayur temple is still in my mind. '*I loved you, oh, Lord of Guruvayur,*' she'd written, '*I came to your door step, but you did not recognise me, I'm in love with the deep dark blue of your body.*' She was a tribal girl, an adivasi.

She used to smoke grass, and so had connections with some grass sellers. I suspect that she was also made a seller. There's every reason to think that her death was related to problems in that trade. She told me once, 'Nalini *chechi*, if I die, you must think of it as a murder. I will never commit suicide.' She'd never tell you what was up, no matter how much you asked. Then once she revealed that she had a child, a lame child. She didn't tell us where the kid was. She used to constantly talk of death to other friends and to me. We thought this was all part of getting high on joints.

Meanwhile, my area of work shifted to Thiruvanantha-puram, with a trip to Thailand. One day in between, when I visited Jwalamukhi, everyone there complained about Ammu. 'She's a terrible nuisance,' they said, 'she's forever picking up a razor blade at the drop of a hat.' She was a bit violent by nature. This happened on 10 September. She'd pay some heed if Sarada or Lalita or I spoke to her seriously. I never had to scold her. She'd become a good girl the moment she saw me. I felt that she might be taking advantage of this, and so gave her a good dressing-down. 'What's your problem?' I asked rather snappily. 'Get out of this place. Don't ever come back!' She replied quickly, and her words were ill-starred. 'No, Nalini *chechi*,' she said. 'You will never see me here again.'

She'd been staying in the loft. She came down in the clothes she'd been wearing and calmly walked out. Usually she'd carry her towel and other things. That didn't happen this time. She died that night. I was at the railway station just next to that spot at that moment. I normally took the Malabar Express or the Guruvayur Express. But that day, I decided to go by the Amrita Express and waited till midnight. It was as if I were caught there and could not leave. I left by Amrita, however, not knowing of the terrible happening.

The police's version of her death claimed she was run over by a train while trying to escape from them. That's a bloody lie. She would never have run even from thugs; she would have faced them with her blade. On that day, three people had taken her away in an auto. There were witnesses who had seen her run, screaming. It's mysterious that even with all this evidence, the police insisted that she was running from them. But of course, it's well known that the police don't usually own up so fast when such things happen.

The corpse was recovered with sword-gashes on it. There was some effort to institute an inquiry into the death. The newspapers weren't interested in following up the investigation. A documentary for a local channel made by two journalists, Sreenivasan and Gopinathan, was telecast. Nothing happened, since the dead person was a sex worker.

Ammu had told us that her mother had died young and that she'd left home unable to bear her stepmother's torture. Her relatives, who had had no contact with her for a long time, came down from Wayanad and declared to the police that they had no complaint; with that the investigation ended. They had neither the ability nor the money to carry on the legal procedure.

This experience taught me how helpless a sex worker is in life. Despite strong evidence, despite the fact that she had known that she'd be murdered and had told many about it, despite being seen by people just before her death, Ammu's murder was erased from the records, on the grounds of 'poor evidence'. No doubt, there was a mafia that worked behind it.

Ammu had taken part in Medha Patkar's agitation against the Sardar Sarovar dam. She and a sex worker called Usha from Thrissur were part of the twenty-five member group that had gone to Delhi to take part in the protest march. The group had gone to Narmada from Delhi and they took part in the agitation there. Ammu had told me about the time she spent there with the struggling adivasis. I can't help remembering, however, an awfully sad side to all this. In Delhi, they had *gheraoed*[1] the Chief Minister of Maharashtra and were arrested. On receiving bail at night, they were put up at the Vivekananda Hall.

In the morning, a woman from the NGO SEWA found

---

[1] Surrounding a person on all sides, as a form of 'besieging in protest'.

her purse missing. She decided that Ammu and Usha had stolen her purse. Some demanded that they should be searched. Others held firm that in that case, everyone should be searched. In the end, everyone's bags were searched but nothing was produced. I too have learnt from experience that the practice of a kind of untouchability which stems from certain prejudices is widely prevalent, and that in this, there's little difference between activists and ordinary people. It's women who strut around thinking of themselves as progressive who often behave the worst.

Women Friends

Another of my co-workers whom I remember with an inward thrill is Sabira. Her performance at a seminar organised by us at Ernakulam was unforgettable. It was the legal experts who mostly spoke on that occasion. The presidents of the State and National Women's Commissions, Sugata Kumari, and Mohini Giri, were speakers as well. Though a few sex workers, including Sabira, had gone there to take part in the seminar, they were refused admission for the technical reason that they hadn't registered earlier. They tried to reach Mohini Giri. The issue was raised through Sugata Kumari.

Shocking the entire audience, Mohini Giri publicly requested the sex workers present there to inaugurate the seminar. Sarojini went up the stage to light the lamp. When Mohini Giri asked one of them to speak, Sabira went up. She was doing so for the first time, but she presented an account of the conditions of our lives and our rights very effectively.

But her concluding remarks were rather unexpected. She ended by asking for help from everyone. When she came out, she said that she'd done that because Justice Janaki Amma, who had been on the dais with her, had requested her to do so. After all, this is a senior lady, she thought, we must respect her wishes.

Later, at Kozhikode, Sabira was arrested and beaten up brutally. Picked up one evening, she was tortured the whole night. Her breasts were infected and filled with pus; she had to undergo surgery at the medical college to get cured. For six whole months, she was entirely bed-ridden. It was after this incident that sex workers took to public protest. As a result, the Human Rights Commission conducted an inquiry.

In October 2004, Sabira expired. That was a parting that plunged all of us in grief. She died at an institution called Snehashraya in Kannur. There's one thing we felt gratified about, though. Before, her body would have been disposed of as an unclaimed corpse in the public cemetery. We took the lead to make a collection to bring her dead body to Kozhikode and lay it to rest according to religious rites.

There are other departures that bring painful memories. Thankamani and Ramani took their own lives. A few days before, we had quarrelled. Ramani had been invited to speak representing Kerala at the sex workers conference at Kolkata. For some reason, they withdrew this offer and extended it to me. Ramani felt insulted at this. We kept fighting until we returned to Kerala. Thankamani and I were on one side and Ramani on the other. We bickered so much; we were a nuisance to the other passengers. It was quite a few days before that squabble ended. Within a few months, both committed suicide. Apparently, it was the fighting in their families that made them do this.

Usha, Thresiamma, Sasikala and others were active in the early days of the organisation at Thrissur. Gradually we extended our activities to Ernakulam and Thiruvanantha-puram. With Maitreyan's and Jayashree's support, we gained national attention. The first get-together at Thiruvanantha-puram sparked off controversies and debates. Later we successfully held a national conference at Ernakulam over-coming many hurdles. The conference put forth many demands like a minimum wage of a hundred rupees for sex workers, concessions for building houses, ration cards, free medical facilities and so on. The activists who were behind all this work included Sarojini, Chandrika, Lila, Thresiamma, Saudamini, Molly, Lalita, Lakshmi, Jameela, Thankamani and Sasikala. Many of these activists were physical wrecks, destroyed by the police brutality we had had to face in the early days. That we were able to check the violence of the police and the local toughs to a large extent remains one of the major gains we secured in this phase.

Among the newer entrants in sex work, Sini was a parti-cularly remarkable person. She helped me a lot with my documentary. In a play we put up recently, called 'One-Night's Darlings', written by Shantakumar, she played the role of a pregnant sex worker. The play ended with the sex worker deciding to raise her child if it were male and to kill it if it were female. Sini was actually pregnant then, pregnant from a client she favoured. She played that character beautifully. She is now a member of the famous playwright P.M. Antony's drama troupe. Another member of the troupe married her in May 2005. She is trying to find a future in theatre.

But no one could match Lizzie of Ernakulam for sheer guts. Her favourite haunt was the railway station. She would carry either chilli powder or a knife most of the time. Her tactic was to pay back the police in their own coin: with chilli powder. Once when two women were arrested, she walked straight into the police station with that fiery weapon of hers, and got them out just by talking tough. The toughest of people would think twice before messing with her. Another time, she removed the roof-tiles of a police station to rescue five women. They escaped but she was caught. She was beaten by the police on several occasions. She's a front-line activist of the organisation.

A sex worker who attracted me in a different sort of way was Anu. She and I had been friends since we worked together in the clay mine. She had been in love, but her family forced her to marry someone else. The husband had a terrible complex as he was dark and she, fair. The kids born to them were fair-skinned, and that led to terrible fights and beatings. Finally she took her children and left with the help of another man. She placed her children in an orphanage and became a sex worker. Once she had a steady income, she brought them back.

Meanwhile, the husband's family, which was going through

a big financial crisis, began to depend on her. The husband's second wife, his older brother's wife, his younger brother's wife and his two sisters joined her. They all live together now like a Company House. They even have a Maruti van to move around in. All of them do sex work. The kids were respectably married off once they grew up. The husband was invited to take the father's privileged place, but he isn't connected to her as her husband anymore.

Prison

Though people gave the Jwalamukhi label to us rather mockingly in the early days, later, it became a symbol of our self-confidence. In many places, I myself have seen policemen quivering at its mention. Once at Guruvayur, twelve sex workers who were waiting for a bus to go for a HIV test, were arrested by sub-inspector Biju Narayanan and his team. I got to know of this, and went to the police station. He asked me why those who do sex work need the HIV test. When the argument grew heated, he got up to kick me. At once a policeman ran to him and whispered that I was a Jwalamukhi. He muttered something under his breath and let off everybody. All this, in five minutes' time.

It was just when Jwalamukhi's activities became wide-spread that I was jailed. The raids in Guruvayur heated up around that time. Sub-inspector Narayanankutty was a die-hard fanatic when it came to pulling up sex workers. Often he'd be in plainclothes. I knew him by sight. One day he came up to me in mufti when I was standing at the bus stop, offered five hundred rupees and asked me whether I'd go with him. I asked where I was to meet him. He told me the place; I told him to walk on, that I'd join him in a moment. The bus to Thrissur stopped there and I escaped, jumping into the bus.

But on another occasion I fell into the police's trap. The policeman asked me who I had come to meet in Guruvayur and I replied, 'S.I. Narayanankutty *saar*.' The fellow had a fit. '*Saar* offered me five hundred that day. I wasn't able to take that offer, so I've come today.' I kept my cool and kept saying this over and over again. He sent me to court. I'd expected the place to be just like in the movies, with the lawyers striding up and down the courtroom and arguing. Nothing of that sort happened. No one asked me a thing and I was packed off to jail, to Viyoor prison. As soon as he saw me, the jailor asked, 'So you are the Jwalamukhi leader?' I didn't suffer the ill-treatment many of my friends had had to face. I can say I had V.I.P treatment. In the evening they invited me to watch a video film they'd borrowed. I stayed there for three days absolutely unharmed. On the fourth day, I was out on bail put up by Paulson and others.

Jayashree

This was the day before Vishu.[2] Jayashree introduced me to Vandana, who was from Orissa. I was introduced as a Jwalamukhi activist, a person who didn't speak much. This was before I'd done some public speaking. For the first time,

---

[2] One of the two most important Hindu festivals in Kerala, which falls in April.

we ate together — usually, we sat separately. Jayashree had everyone sit around the same table. I was still apprehensive. This was often a ploy used by some women in the PSH project to butter us up.

I got closer to Jayashree at the seminar at Thrissur. I could see by then that she wasn't allergic to sex workers. Then we went together to a meeting at Chennai to form an organisation called the Indian Sex Workers' Forum. The decisions taken there were translated into Tamil and announced. I disagreed with many of these, feeling that sex workers weren't being given enough importance. I said so. Jayashree asked me to go on stage and share my views. Though I'd got over stage fright somewhat, I was still very timid, and not at all confident. When I pointed out that sex workers didn't seem to have much importance in the sex workers' forum, there was enthusiastic clapping from the audience. Jayashree too was thrilled to bits by this. After that I began to regularly accompany her wherever she went. We travelled together to Kolkata on the organisation's business. We used to be very proud that we had a doctor (Jayashree's a trained doctor) with us.

We went to Kolkata again when the Kolkata Sex Workers' Forum celebrated March 3 as Indian Sex Workers' Day. Everyone there was recounting the miseries and the harassment they faced. I put forward some other views, trying to argue that sex workers were different from other women. Answering the question how, I mentioned four points. We are free in four respects. We don't have to cook and wait for a husband; we don't have to wash his dirty clothes; we don't have to ask for our husbands' permission to raise our kids as we deem fit; and we don't have to run after our husbands claiming rights to their property to raise our kids. Instead of endlessly lamenting our sorry plight back home in the five minutes we got to speak, I thought it more satisfying to advance these views.

In most places where Jayashree spoke for us, she had to face questions from many people, including her friends. They used to tell her that she wasn't a sex worker and that sex workers' affairs were quite unlike what she made them out to be. On these occasions, she would encourage me to speak up. That's how I picked up the ability to make my points myself.

Jayashree's friendliness was not limited to me. There were some among us who weren't that clean. Often, when people like Ammu came close, many would shrink back. Jayashree never did this. Indeed, she believed that a bath every day wasn't necessary at all! Jayashree stood by us as we built our organisation; but beyond that she also shares a life with us. Paulson and Maitreyan too are like this, but that a woman was ready to do this touched us deeply.

The Journey to Thailand

For about four years, I travelled regularly. After I worked on my first documentary, I went to Thailand to screen it along with Jayashree and Reshma Bharadwaj. Jayashree used to take care to see that what I said was faithfully communicated.

I've travelled to Mumbai, Chennai, Delhi and Andhra

Pradesh along with Jayashree. We went to Kolkata together four times. The first trip to Thailand was made possible through Jayashree's acquaintance with Vandana. I attended a training programme that helped sex workers develop the skills to deal with their problems themselves. But for this, the Kolkata people would have been given priority. They are a 65,000-strong organisation.

Paulson and Lalita came along with me on the first journey. This was a Media and Social Workshop organised by the Global Alliance against Traffic in Women. Problems began right from getting the passport. I thought it would be enough to go to the passport office and tell them my name and date of birth.

But there I was told that I needed a ration card. When I got married, the first thing Father had done was to get my name erased from our ration card. He knew that it was very important. I thought, well, they've lost the two-and-a-half measures of rice and sugar allotted to me, that's all. I didn't feel that I'd lost my very identity! However, after some persistence, I did get my passport.

I was so excited about taking that flight. To fly in an aeroplane had been one of my life's ambitions. Maitreyan gave me the tickets and I got into the plane. I wasn't thinking then about going some place to learn camera work; my thoughts were all about how I was stepping into a plane and flying to some distant place. I was in a different world. Each step led me towards a dream world!

Once I reached there, the camera became a great wonder.

You should see one of my early learning cassettes. It's great fun — I started off not even knowing how to capture the image of the person standing right in front of me, but with time I captured the entire country in it! After learning how to handle the camera, we made a three-minute film by ourselves. You had to come up with an original concept for this.

My concept had three central characters — a well-off young man, a well-off 'society lady' and then, me. The 'society lady' and me were both asking a favour of this young man in two different ways. I ask for help as a beggar. He hands me the smallest change he has. The other woman asks him for some money saying that she's lost her purse. He pulls out dollars and counts them out to her. Don't they say that men lavish money on women they desire? Well, here I'm in the role of a pretty woman. But his attitude is pretty much the same. I can't really express in words the sheer thrill I felt when I translated that idea into film!

Besides us from India, there were participants from Cambodia, Nepal, Bangladesh and other countries. A Malaysian couple, who were committed to training sex workers in camera work, were in charge of the programme. The first few days were devoted to discussions. Then for seven days, we were trained to use the camera. We were also given video cameras at the end of the programme.

I went to Thailand the third time in 2004. This time, it was Jayanti who came with me. I was there to screen the second documentary I'd made and to participate in the discussions. This time some disagreements cropped up between the organisers and me. I didn't like their suggestion that my third work should focus on police atrocities. I felt that it was more important to highlight the negative attitude of the public. Jayanti translated this quite effectively. Nor did I like being confined to or limited by the experience of being a sex worker. I stated openly that I didn't need their camera or their money if I wasn't allowed to work on the theme I preferred. Though they weren't convinced, they finally allowed this.

There were some refreshingly different experiences on this journey. One of Jayanti's friends, a Malayali girl living there, used to come every day and take us around town in her car on sight-seeing and shopping trips. She was an ordinary housewife. I will never forget how she was ready to interact closely with me, out of the pride she felt that a Malayali woman, and that too a sex worker, had become the director of a documentary. In all the documentaries shown there, mine earned the greatest attention. She and her husband were there at the airport to bid us goodbye when we left. I consider this a great recognition.

Paulson Raphael and Maitreyan

Paulson and Maitreyan had entirely different styles of activism. If Paulson was with you, he would advise you, give you his opinion that it would be more effective if you said it that way or this way. On the contrary, Maitreyan enjoyed whatever we said and let us say whatever we pleased. That way we could end up saying foolish things. But since there was no insistence on what 'line' to take, we had the courage to speak up on anything that looked relevant to us. We also got a chance to evaluate the strong points and the blunders we had made in our words and deeds.

Paulson was more firm in his suggestions and was particular about pointing out our insights and our errors strongly and on the spot. His nature was to make sure that we secured whatever we aimed for. There was no chance for compromise. Maitreyan wasn't like that. He's pretty cool even when things don't turn out as expected. He took the position that it was okay to keep silent sometimes. Both of them contributed to my self-confidence, though in different ways.

It's at Maitreyan's and Jayashree's house that my daughter stayed most often when I was shifting residence or going on trips. When accompanying Maitreyan, it was an unsaid rule that we must not behave badly, and that we must see others just as we see ourselves. Paulson wasn't like that. With him, you didn't have to be cautious; you were free to say anything bluntly to anyone.

Paulson made some crucial interventions in my life. When I got the chance to go to Thailand, someone in our office did something deliberately to obstruct the issuing of my passport. This was done with the belief that he would go instead of me. Though this person was Paulson's good friend and colleague, he still stood up firmly for me. That was why I managed to go. After studying for his Master's in social work in Delhi, Paulson went to Sonagacchi and other places in Kolkata and got to know of the sex workers' organisation, and it was this experience that convinced him that he should stand alongside the abandoned. He was willing to stand firmly for issues no one had bothered about before, and leave, allowing all the credit for the good work done to go to others. He never tried to let people know what he had done.

Maitreyan had this way of openly saying things anywhere and before anyone. When we had disagreements with the government on the implementation of the AIDS project, there was an argument with the Minister for Health, P. Sankaran. Asked what they did, Maitreyan pulled out a wooden model of an erect penis and a condom from his bag, proceeded to carry out a demonstration, and then said, 'This is what we teach people to do.'

Maitreyan openly declared that he was withdrawing from public activism; before this, Paulson changed his field of action without making any declaration. We can never forget that their support and leadership sustained us greatly. Many asked: 'With this, will not the sex workers' movement come to a standstill?' Our struggle for survival did not begin because of individuals; nor can it be given up because of their absence. It's folks who can't stand us or our organisation who ask such childish questions.

Sujata and Raj Thomas

Sujata worked as the finance officer of the PSH project run by Jwalamukhi. She was also a social worker. Though much younger than me, she used to support and encourage me with everything. She was always urging me to stand up in front and speak out. It was my interaction with her that gave me the courage to put together a paper for the Thrissur symposium. She would explain things to me as if she were a teacher.

Raj Thomas, who also worked on the project, helped me a lot. He was the one who shaped my first stray jottings into a proper article and had it published in the Jwalamukhi bulletin. He was a good singer of folk songs and a director of plays; besides, he was also an actor, orator, and a worker in the Marxist party. He had acted in the film *Kuttappan Sakshi*. Though not great to look at, he had all-round talents. But financial problems never gave him peace. I was close to him, and always felt free to discuss everything. He took his own life; we still don't know why. His body was found in a rundown well at his home in Adaat. If he were alive, he would have been my right hand in writing this autobiography. Now I'm supported best by Subhash and Jyotikumar, who both work at FIRM, the organisation with which I'm closely associated these days.

My Daughter's Wedding

My first journey to Thailand had a considerable impact on my daughter. Around that time, things had begun to sour in the household where she was staying. The daughter-in-law was complaining that I was making a lot of money and that my daughter had a good portion of it but would not spend it. So I put her up in one of Shahulkka's relatives' place while I was away. When I returned from Thailand, the TV was showing news of a sex worker being feted. Though I had hinted at my profession earlier, to have it emerge in the open was a major revelation to all of them. When I wrapped up my press conference and returned home, they were watching me on TV. My daughter was worried about the reactions that might follow.

So I took her away from there and went off to Salamat Nagar again. After my illness, except for occasional meetings, we had hardly gone there. I knew there was no TV there, and was sure the new word, *laingikatozhilali* (sex worker), would be gibberish to people there. But the problem there was that many men who had once called me a 'sister' now tried to become my lovers. It became clear that it wouldn't be easy to leave my daughter somewhere and go to work. My sex work stopped, so did my part-time organisational work. It was a most unstable situation; we didn't know where to stay! Then a sudden thought struck me: why not arrange for my daughter's marriage? What I hoped was that, though we weren't rich, since we were Muslims, there'd be someone who would marry her on that consideration.

At Salamat Nagar, someone approached us with a marriage proposal from the Male Islands. We were taken for such a ride in this affair. The passport and a certificate issued by a mosque in Male offered details of the groom, but we discovered later than he was ten years older than either document indicated. I was so afraid that my daughter would recieve no other wedding proposal now that my organisational activity and sex work had become public knowledge that I agreed to the alliance and the marriage.

My daughter hadn't let go of her father in her heart of hearts. Though I had never claimed him, I did not feel the need to declare that she didn't have a father or that he had dumped us. But the question, 'Where's her father?' arose in many situations. I used to say, she has only me, and we can proceed only if you can accept that. Many withdrew their proposals — one reason why I arranged this marriage and sent her off to Male. Admitting that I was a sex worker was less difficult than declaring that my daughter had no father.

Even the Male fellow became adamant once the wedding agreement was finalised. From the wedding agreement to the henna ceremony, I was the sole organiser. There's a practice called 'tannoliyil nikah'[3] which I suggested. Everyone became very sentimental at this point. 'Her father is close by,' they said, 'why not call him?' I too thought, maybe I'm imposing my opinion on her. I had a videographer, and the wedding was a grand affair. But the absence of her father, I thought, was gnawing at my daughter, though she said nothing about it. So, I went hunting for her father on the eve of the wedding, and brought him there, literally laying a trap for him the way they do in Hindi films. He arrived just before the henna ceremony.

My daughter was in Male for about a year — I thought she would visit only on occasion. I began to make very active public appearances in support of our organisation. A year

---

[3]   Usually it is the father or brother who conducts the nikaah, but in the absence of these relatives, the marriage may be conducted by the woman herself. This is referred to as *tannoli*, which means, 'Own voice'.

later, upsetting all my calculations, my daughter returned, turning her back on both the marriage and her husband. Apparently, he had a two-storey house with his own bakery on the ground floor — he actually needed my daughter as a sales-girl for the bakery. She was made to work there without a moment's rest or enough food. In Male, women have more value and status than men. This man's family, however, was from Kerala, so it was just the reverse. To him the wife was only a slave. He would not let her visit her own place. In the end, she concocted some pretext to leave and escaped with her life. She would never go back.

Her return was a great challenge to me. I had begun to figure prominently in the media by then, so I was widely recognised. Finding a place for my daughter to stay became a huge problem. At first, I turned to Maitreyan. But his house was always full of people; she couldn't stay there very long. Then began another merry-go-round, moving from house to house: Indira's place, the home for sex workers' kids, the Chilla, Reshma's, then my niece's place.

That second phase was truly a trial because my daughter was now once-married, thought of as likely to run off with anyone. An image that had always been there, now became permanent. It became impossible to find a home where she could stay for very long.

This brought about some very positive changes in Zeenat. She became quite fearless, bold enough to face press reporters and take part in public functions. Her stay with Jayashree gave her a lot of spirit. From harbouring a lurking feeling that her Amma was doing something wrong, she came under the influence of people who accepted her Amma. She saw that Nalini's daughter would never be abandoned, that she would be accepted. That made her self-confidence grow by leaps and bounds. Before this, her usual practice had been to stay passive in moments of crisis, simply shutting her eyes to the world. Her interaction with the sex workers from Kolkata taught her many things.

In the Bangladesh Colony

I decided to settle in Kozhikode after I went for a meeting there. I set up house in Santi Nagar in the Bangladesh Colony in 2004, and have lived there ever since. My daughter began working as a door-to-door salesperson, along with another female friend. She wanted to earn something on her own, even if it wasn't much.

Sudheer, an autorickshaw driver, liked her a lot and proposed marriage. She was in a state of mind where marrying anyone from India meant doom to her! So initially she refused the offer. But when she learned that he'd proposed knowing everything about me and about her first marriage, she began to relent. In Bangladesh Colony, too, she was living along with the children of sex workers; that gave her a lot of fortitude. Here too, owning up to being Nalini's daughter only made her stronger. We had no reason to hide our name or our roots.

There were some objections, but we overcame them and the wedding finally took place, bringing me great peace and calm in its wake. My son-in-law is educated and has studied up to the undergraduate level. He accepts me and understands me. The fact that he accompanied my daughter to a public function soon after their wedding in which eunuchs, sex workers and gays joined in made me immensely happy.

A girl who walks out of a marriage has the same problems as a girl who isn't married. No one feels confident about accommodating her. After my daughter returned from Male, I stayed at a rented house in Thiruvananthapuram for a year. The woman who leaves her marriage is stigmatised as a 'man-eater', someone on the prowl for men all the time. In all honesty, we left Kozhikode because it wasn't possible to leave her alone at home. And because of that, she married well. Things have been smooth, till now. What else can we say?

People in Thiruvananthapuram look at the Poonthura-Beemappalli area as if it is bristling with dangers. The people in these two areas have given each other a hard time, with a lot of violence breaking out between the two areas time and again. I have lived there. My experience is that the people there are better than others. I can say the same thing about the Bangladesh Colony. From the outside, it looks notorious. Kids from that area don't get jobs in decent places, people don't treat them well – you tell anyone that you're from there and, well, the impression is, as we say, that you are a 'gone case', beyond salvation. But I have never felt so secure anywhere. Since we are all 'gone cases', outsiders don't bother us, and all of us insiders get on very well with a lot of mutual cooperation and affection.

There was a new Prohibition Committee in Bangladesh Colony which served free rice porridge as lunch for some months. I was always at odds with them. You know why? I know perfectly well that hooch distilling doesn't happen at Bangladesh Colony. There are two ways in which liquor is sold there. One way is to buy a couple of bottles from the wholesale shop with a proper bill written up and then retail it in small quantities. That brings around fifty rupees as profit per bottle. There are small families that survive on this. Some people manage to sell up to two bottles a day. The other way is to get 'duplicate' liquor from Mangalore, which is sold as military liquor.

It was in such an area that the prohibition people kept having meetings and protests. What was there to prohibit in this area? Shouldn't they do away with the wholesale shops, try their enforcement there? Shouldn't they prohibit bar licences? What's the use of preaching prohibition in an area where people manage to sell barely four bottles of liquor a day? I've seen the same liquor being served in a VIP area just next door to us when I went to a wedding.

Of course, there was the question of free distribution of rice porridge. Half of that was up to the government to organise, the other half with the prohibition committee. One day my son-in-law's mother went to get us some; she asked for rice porridge for four people, which included me. 'Nalini can't be given porridge,' they told her. 'She's not from this place.' Well, isn't it a fact that I sought refuge here because I'm destitute? What sort of a government is this, which says it can't give me porridge?

There are other rules, besides. If you want some porridge, you had better queue up, even if you are a tiny little kid. What's poured is charity; there are iron-clad rules on how to accept charity! Then the houses that ask for the porridge are given numbers, and these are written down on paper and put up on the walls too! After that you've to take a card to collect your porridge. Some cards are for five, some for three – my foot, will anyone go begging for this unless they are so, so hard up? Along with the porridge, you also get Bengal gram and other lentils — not the good wholesome green gram but the flaccid red gram with no vitamins, nothing, which no one wants.

But the best part of the story came later. These very fellows who'd not give me porridge, the very same chaps, served me lentil vadas and chutney on the day I filmed the first meeting of the Prohibition Committee. Oh, how they coaxed me, 'Madam, please eat!'

We may be able to return the favour by serving rice instead of porridge. But to do that is also mockery. It's like rushing off to kill a child the moment you've heard that someone's killing a cow. If they weren't so helpless, people would have flatly refused to take this, just out of self-respect. The porridge that used to be served to over a hundred people is now served to just about thirty.

What's surprising is that people say that sex work is worse than being on the dole like this. 'We'll give you work,' they say. What work are they going to give us? It's people who can't give work to the healthy and educated people queuing up for jobs who make these promises!

This is just what's going to happen in this effort to resettle sex workers. They'll be dragged off to some area like this and put on the dole. Like they did to the beggars. Build a shed for men, women and kids, a long shed in which you'll get wet when the wind blows during the monsoon. There was such a shed in Guruvayur. I've stayed there once. Caged up in a dog's house; that's what I call this rounding up of people all inflicted with various scourges!

The Bangladesh Colony was formed when homeless people got together to put up their little huts. They were people who earned nothing. Then people got some sex workers from the town to live there. When they went off to make money at night, these people would care for their kids, wash their clothes, and offer space to rest. Thus the residents there are of two sorts — the ones who came first, and the later ones who were brought there. Then the sex workers began to put up houses. Only rarely have they bought houses. That's how this became a colony.

Hashish came there very recently. When it became impossible to sell it in town, it began to be sold from houses here. In this trade, a few became rich and the rest stayed as miserable as ever. That brought unevenness, a sense of the well-off and the worse-off, and that's how the Bangladesh Colony got split in two. When seventeen people died because some poison had been added to the grass, these became yawning differences. In the southern part, drugs were not sold very openly. In the northern side, at the time I went there, people used to queue up for it. This created jealousy and the politicians influenced the other side and beat these people up. Some houses were wrecked. Actually, all the politicians were involved in this. There was also the large-scale drug lobby that worked behind all this. When these small operators began to make profits, they began to get the stuff from places outside. So it became imperative for the big ones to beat three or four families to the ground.

The visual media fellows thrust themselves into several houses on this pretext to do their shooting. The gall! Who gave them permission? In the name of reporting the drug trade, they barged like animals into the house of Sarojini, a sex worker. That was outright bestial. There were four mature young women in that house. It's into that house that a bunch of men forced themselves in one day, rampaging as far as the bathroom. What if one of those girls had been there, taking a bath?

The local boys threw stones at them. Which person with self-respect wouldn't do that? The lads did this because they loved their sisters. The police are only guard dogs. They also got their share of the stone throwing. The police beat our lads black and blue.

CHAPTER FIVE

The Girl who Welcomed AKG

When my Valyachan's son was shot by a Congress worker, AKG and Susheela Gopalan[1] came to pay him a visit. I was selected to welcome them with tender coconut. There they sat, next to each other, in wooden chairs. Those days we had only kerosene lamps in our houses so we had lit an oil-lamp and placed it on the floor. Valyachan's house had a low ceiling, like in most old-style houses. They are there still in my mind as if in a portrait: AKG extending his arms to accept the tender coconut, the pinkish glow on Susheela Gopalan's pretty, fair-skinned face. She was wearing a traditional sari of a colour that was neither coffee nor black. I was dressed up like the heroines of Malayalam ballads, with the sari wrapped around my chest, some of my hair tied up in a knot on the side of my head with red silk thread, and tresses streaming over my shoulder. I carried that image of me for a long time. The image of the girl who welcomed AKG.

Around that time, I unwittingly became the leader of a strike. When I first went to work, the pay was two rupees. I asked for two-and-a-half, and declared that we wouldn't come to work if we weren't paid that much. 'You don't have to come,' the

---

[1] The most beloved of all communist leaders in Kerala, A.K. Gopalan, and his wife, Susheela, who was also a prominent activist and later, leader of the Communist Party.

boss retorted, 'from tomorrow, none of you will have jobs here.'
Well, I took him seriously. The women I went to work with used
to come by my house with their baskets in the morning. I told
them all, 'We don't have work.'

But that turned into a revolt. All the men had turned up.
The women in my team didn't come. The people at the worksite
thought I'd done as I said, as I was a political activist's daughter.
I didn't know a thing about politics then. But something in my
mind told me that I should do as I say. So for some time, I was
everybody's leader.

There's a picture from before this time that remains very
clear in my mind. At the age of eleven, I too took part in a
demonstration as part of a struggle to occupy surplus land. 'Give
us land, give us land, give us land to farm paddy and tapioca!'
Those were the slogans. The feeling that I was a person worthy
of attention overwhelmed me as I walked along raising slogans
and holding the flag aloft. Like we say, a 'brave warrior woman'!
When I saw people staring from the roadside, I shouted slogans
all the more loudly. Only later did I understand that people were
staring because I was beautiful! Though I was only eleven, my
body was as mature as a fourteen-year-old's. I was clad in a
short knee-length skirt and a half-sleeved blouse. That was to
later become Silk Smitha's costume.[2] That was what we had
those days, when it came to clothes.

There was an old woman who came with us on the march.
When she came home, she used to be served rice porridge in

---

[2] A popular actress who was known for her sexy screen appearances.

a leaf placed over a hole dug in the ground. She'd inevitably slit the bottom of the leaf as she drank it up. 'Let's serve her in our veranda,' I'd say. Father wouldn't agree. And remember, he wasn't just a communist, he was also a follower of Sree Narayana Guru.

Mother

It's fourteen years since Mother died. I had stopped seeing her many years before that. Losing her job had made her lose all control over life. After that, Father, and later, my older brother, made all the decisions.

From the time I could remember, my mother used to be well-dressed, in a traditional sari, with a sandal mark on her forehead, her long hair lying loose on her shoulders. When our troubles began, she would often cry. Father used to beat her when he was in a temper. She'd weep then too. When Valyamma scolded her, Father would never stand up for her. Now I have a feeling that Father was deeply influenced by my aunt. Maybe that was out of respect for his elder brother's wife. She was also a sexy woman. That could also have been why she influenced him so much.

When I gave birth to my first child by Subbarettan, Mother came in secret to take care of my delivery. Those days she was earning a little something from a temporary job teaching the kids who came to work at the mill. She'd get out of the house on that pretext and come over to care for me.

After I became a sex worker, I used to go to meet her in secret. She would never accept any money I offered her. In her mind, the money earned from sex work was saturated with sin. She'd ask me if the chain I was wearing was of gold. When I replied that it was gold plated, and not pure gold, she'd advise me to save up the money and buy gold so that it would be of use to my children later. When she heard that I was supporting my kids, she advised me to give them only what they needed and save the rest for myself; she said my kids wouldn't love me.

The secret visits also came to an end soon. My brother had married before me. When his wife began to rule the house, Mother was not allowed to go out alone. His daughter would accompany her everywhere, reporting who she met. That made it impossible for us to meet. I couldn't see her even when she died.

I had my picture first taken when I was twenty-one. I wore a traditional sari in it. When I looked at it, it was a lot like Mother's photo. Not like mine! There was an enlarged photograph of Mother in a black blouse and a traditional sari in the house. I, however, had put on a red blouse and red dot on my forehead. Both looked black in the photo!

Mother put that dot on her forehead just for the picture. Usually she never wore one. She'd given birth to nine children at a very young age. Three died; she had to raise the other six. When Father didn't have a job, Mother endured dire poverty and misery. I've never seen her with a dot on her forehead; on rare occasions like Onam, she'd wear some sandal paste. The face decorated with the dot, that was just for the picture. That's why I had the same feeling when I saw my own picture.

Satyan's Dead!

The first movie I went to was *Kaattutulasi*. I was fourteen and it made me sad for two reasons. One, the story was a sad one; two, I got a solid thrashing from Father. A character in that film sings a sad song: 'A Gandharva from the land of the Ganga, once he came by this way....' I thought that what happened later in the film was the *aram* — that's the evil that hits one directly as an effect of one's speaking of that sort of evil — of that song. I sighed to my brother, how terrible this *aram* was, that made the film such a sad one! My brother pooh-poohed this. 'You dumbo,' he said, 'this is not *aram*, this is how the movie was *made*.'

I went to the movies because I was eager to do all that the boys did. Chettan would come back from the movie, *Nallatanka*, and tell us the story. The impression I got from his narration was that the movies were like drama, that is, things happen for real on stage. When Chettan said, 'Satyan died,' I'd ask him, 'Oh, there'll be no more shows, then? Now that he's gone, how can there be a show?' He'd say, 'The next show's at nine.' When we went to see that show, Satyan died: all over again! Chettan was irked; he said, 'You are a big dumb idiot; I'm not taking you to the movies anymore!' We'd gone off to the movies in secret, at night, opening the north-side door of the house. Father didn't know even when we sneaked back in. But when we began to argue over the story, Father woke up. My brother and I, we were always arguing over something or the other. I always insisted that I won; I *had* to win. Chettan usually gave in, but that day he too was determined to win. So the cat was out of the bag, and a sound thumping followed.

Another movie I liked was the one in which Mammooty recovers from cancer through a natural cure, *Sukrtam*. I saw it when I was ill myself.

The discussion we held about T.V. Chandran's film *Susanna*, under the auspices of Jwalamukhi in the Thrissur town hall, attracted a lot of public attention. There we welcomed the director T.V. Chandran and Vani Viswanath, who had played Susanna in the film, and gave them mementos. They said this was the most important award they'd ever got. We voiced our opinions about the film, along with Sara Joseph. I argued that Susanna's world was one of freedom.

Whose Bangle?

Ottanthullal was an art form I had watched in the temple and liked. One person holds up a cloth and sings. Another person acts out the song. There's a lot of joking, at the right moments. Though I didn't know much about art, I did see that this form could be used to make fun of people. You can talk of anything, provided there's a right moment to bring it into the story. I like the *thullal* actor because he is a person who can say things that can't normally be said.

I was always shy about public speaking or any kind of public performance. Whether it was Kaikottikali or Onakkali,[3] I didn't know even a single step. That diffidence left me only after I started making speeches. In my youth, girls who didn't know the Onakkali were looked down upon as somewhat inferior.

---

[3] Group dances performed by women on festive or ritual occasions.

Even when she was convinced that I had had enough of school, Valyamma was very keen to have me trained in Onakkali and Kaikottikali. It was thought to be a sign of aristocracy.

Singing was regarded the same way. I've read poems like *Ramanan* when I was young. Never sung it, though! I read *Ramanan* and *Karuna* because those were the books Father used to read. Then I also read the tuneful verse of *Patinaluvrittam* and the *Irupattinaluvrittam*. In the *Irupattinaluvrittam*, there is a scene in which an *asura* comes to Krishna and implores him for refuge. I remember a few lines here and there, but I still cannot sing them in tune. The same thing goes for *Ramanan*. A few parts stay alive in my mind, as if written there, like the part that begins, 'Flower-decked woods abound...', and 'To tend goats in the shade of the wood....' But I simply can't sing them in tune.

From *Karuna*, it's the part about Vasavadatta's dressing up and the swishing of her robes that stays in my mind. That line about 'waving, so that the delicate bangles jingle...', I was in doubt about that. 'Whose bangle was it, Vasavadatta's or her companion's? The person who wrote this doesn't know much,' I'd think. 'Do bangles jingle when one waves? Such delicate bangles? Really?'

Nalini, Jameela

I lost faith in God somewhere between the ages of nine and twelve. When Mother lost her job and was running around to somehow get it back, it was I who always accompanied her. Actually, it's my older brother who should've gone. But he was always a little withdrawn. So Mother used to prefer my company on all her trips. On the way back, Mother would pray at Krishna's temple to get her job back. Then we'd get down at a place called Nayarangadi. There's a Siva temple there. We'd be late, and Father would be waiting for us on the road. Father was a Party man, so there wasn't a hierarchy in our walking — he wouldn't insist on walking in front of Mother. They'd be walking side-by-side and then when the temple came close, she'd slowly step back and pray. I used to be most amused by this. Why be scared of Father when you're praying to Siva? Who's more powerful? Father or Siva? When I see a temple even now, I remember this.

I can't say I have no faith at all. There was the time I took refuge in the mosque, during a very bad illness. In those periods of helplessness, drinking sanctified water, praying with a peacock feather in my hair – all these rituals were very comforting.

So often it was the mosque that gave me refuge; it was the alms I received there that kept me alive. So I also had the fear that believing outright that there was no God would invite divine retribution. I have had no experience that would make me declare that there's God for sure. But I was scared to say that God didn't exist. In the mosques, girls get kidnapped, raped, harassed, those who come to carry out vows are beaten if they don't pay bribes – if there were a God, would such things happen? The things that happen in the Yerwadi mosque, they are worse. It's common to dump people there as mad folk just to get rid of them in property disputes. If these people don't receive justice in God's own house, what's the point of talking of God? If I had had an experience that revealed to me God's strength in my three-and-a-half years of misery, I would have become a staunch believer. Not once did any such event happen.

It was during my illness that a practitioner of the occult gave me a total of around five thousand rupees over the course of several meetings. Many people had advised me to go to meet this chap to get rid of my illness. I'm ready to try everything, so I went. This tumour used to bulge out of my middle. I went there bathed and clean with my hair unbound. 'You've come dressed well,' he said. This was to build my inner strength, I surmised. There's a particular worship there on the day of the asterism, *ayilyam*, that involves pouring turmeric water on your head. Pots of turmeric water, sometimes seven, sometimes eleven, would be poured over you. You sit in a place on the side of the house where a drain discreetly lets the water out. I didn't know anything of their rules and requirements. So I hadn't taken anything to change into.

He gave me a *lungi* to wear during the worship. There was a place there where you could change. I didn't have a blouse to wear over the *lungi*. I didn't think it was a great problem, so I wore the *lungi* over my chest. A little sacred statue was put into my hands and water poured on my head. While he was pouring the water, he stroked my shoulders. When this was repeated, I understood. Then when I changed after the pouring and went back in, he pulled out a five-hundred-rupee-note and three hundred-rupee-notes from inside a little jar into which he usually crumpled the notes. People hand him notes in this crumpled way. So I thought it must be some sacred amulet!

Maybe he had made a mistake, I thought. So I told him, '*Saar*, this is money.' He just shook his head. I could tell then and there, this was a 'gone case'. It was good fun to hear him chant. He'd chant some verses in Sanskrit and then say, 'Please rescue this tulsi plant from the thorns.' This would be in raw Malayalam. We too were made to pray this way. I was asked to go a second time, and I went. This way of sneaking me hundred rupee notes became regular. Since he met people in two different places, a board saying 'Not Home' would be hung. The major worship would all be conducted at home. The other place was merely for consultations and fixing appointments for worship at home. One day, I was told to be there at the other place.

Usually what he wanted was very normal — the standard sort of sex. The money would come even if this didn't happen. When I went there another time, another person had also been asked to come. Probably his memory had slipped. I'd gone there and was lying on a makeshift bed laid out after removing the inky water he used for his divination. When the bell rang, I was taken into the room for worship. I thought the person who had come was his wife: she was a stunningly beautiful woman. The worship-room was somewhat dark. He took her to the divination-bedroom, then came out of it, shut the door, and let me out. That woman didn't know I was in there.

Perhaps all occult-experts are not like this. Whatever the case, this experience completely changed my impression of them.

As a person newly converted to Islam, I used to enjoy a degree of friendly help. It was just that it varied from place to place. In Malappuram, there are many places where the poor are given help. They don't make fun of you in such places with questions like, 'Aren't you healthy? Why can't you work?' In the three-and-a-half years when I didn't do sex work, I used to get alms not just from the mosque but also from going house-to-house. This is called 'going to collect *sadka*' and is considered to be a bit higher than begging for alms. Saying that you were a new convert brought you more. People would behave well and give you special attention.

I stayed for sometime with Shahulkka at Malappuram. This was when his wife went to the Gulf. He had abandoned me; I stayed in various mosques at that time, and in his relatives' house. He wanted to settle things with me, and I chose Malappuram as the place to live in. He rented a house in secret and Zeenu and I lived there. Shahulkka would come in the day. I was not his wife any more, but we had to maintain a public face. What was funny was that people became curious about our family life. Zeenu was asked often when her father and mother 'got together' since Shahulkka came during the day. She of course couldn't understand what 'getting together' was. After Shahulkka left me and I was stuck there, the people around gave me food and clothes. People returning from the Gulf would give me new clothing material.

In Malappuram, people also promised help to marry off my girl. I decided against that. She was just fourteen then. It was the Jamaat-e-Islam which offered help. If we accepted, she would have to wear the purdah. She wasn't a complete believer, either. Besides, she wasn't the sort who'd come out of the faith if she wanted to. I decided I wouldn't throw her into a place from which she'd never be able to return. They had promised twenty-five sovereigns of gold.

I have never walked around as a Muslim with a sari over my head twenty-four hours a day. But when in the company of relatives, I used to be the most disciplined believer. And I didn't make a decision to stay away from them, ever.

I took the name Jameela after living with Shahulkka for some time. Once when a policeman asked my name, I told him it was Jameela. Another policeman who heard this butted in and said, 'You are lying, isn't your name Nalini?' Those who knew me still knew me as Nalini. So I decided: let my name be Nalini Jameela.

Media Ties

Though the media was generally hostile to us in the early days of our organisation, gradually our experiences began to catch their eye. Jwalamukhi's activities used to get reported in the papers and magazines. When we had a meeting in Chennai, *Nakkeeran* published a report.

At that time, some dramatic turns in the *Nattarangu* discussion programme on the Asianet TV channel caught public attention. The discussion was about the problems of women. When a sex worker said that we too had husbands and kids and that many of us had adopted kids, the Panchayat member, a Congress leader, claimed that we wanted to make the children sex workers in the future and that was why we had adopted them. That was infuriating, and he was made to apologise right there. That woman had adopted a boy.

The first visual media programme I took part in was Asianet's *Akattalam*, in its seventy-seventh episode. Maitreyan had introduced me as a health worker as he feared that I might be denied the opportunity if my identity as a sex worker was revealed. Vinaya,[4] who has put up a strong resistance against male dominance, was also a participant. Vinaya demanded that I reveal my true identity. The topic of discussion was 'Women and the Police'. When a senior police officer claimed that they never harassed sex workers, I opposed him with evidence. I cited an incident which had happened just a day earlier in which twenty-six sex workers had been arrested in Thrissur and put behind bars in Kozhikode. This was apparently provoked by the fact that a sex worker had stood next to a magistrate's wife at the KSRTC bus stand. This was thought of as an insult and twenty-six people had been seized from various parts of the town. To my question about the crime for which they had been arrested, he had no reply.

I also described another incident that had happened in Thrissur. This had happened to an art student, Anto, in a police lock-up. Telling the students that this was what they deserved, the sub-inspector had taken a handful of chilli powder and thrown it into the eyes of many sex workers who were also in the lock-up.

Throughout this discussion, Vinaya and I had to keep confronting others. Vinaya's opinion that policewomen should

---

[4] Vinaya is a well-known women's rights activist in Kerala, a young policewoman who has been in the limelight for her struggle for the rights of policewomen, and against the male authorities in the police force.

not wear a sari and should take to pants and shirts like men led to a lot of heated exchanges. When asked, 'How would you go to the loo in pants?' she retorted, 'How did they manage to empty their bowels wearing pants?' When it was remarked that if women wore pants, men would get aroused, she said that she too got excited when she saw men without shirts.

In this matter, personally, I differ from Vinaya. I think that femininity is a woman's strength. There is not much advantage in aping men, having short hair and wearing pants. I've been intimate with many, many men and so I know well that they aren't that free. So there's no point in being like them.

Then the other big TV programme I took part in was Sun TV's *Kathayalla, Nijam*. The film actress, Lakshmi, was the anchor. She got in touch with me after reading a news item about the hotel run by Jwalamukhi in Thrissur published in the *Nakkeeran*. The shooting was at Chennai and I got VIP treatment throughout. I was put up in a five star hotel, quite an unexpected experience. Lakshmi was prepared to hear me through, without any of the airs of being a big actress. Because of that I was able to say all that I wanted to say quite effectively.

Then later when I appeared on Asianet News Hour, there was the question about what I was doing to end sex work. I replied that my desire was to maintain it. Many did not like this. But since this was a live programme, it couldn't be edited.

CHAPTER SIX

Rehabilitation

A question often raised with regard to sex workers, especially in Kerala, is that of our 'rehabilitation'. Many have asked me whether the world-famous spiritual lady, Mata Amritanandamayi, doesn't endorse this. I want to ask these people whether they have ever tried to find out about sex workers' family ties, social ties. Is it possible to build afresh their domestic ties and social ties through rehabilitation? Won't this merely leave the sex worker all the more isolated and helpless?

What's meant by rehabilitation? Sex workers may be shifted to a different place, but is it possible to keep sustaining them? 'Sex workers' doesn't refer to a group that stays the same all the time. These are people who keep changing. If some move out, others move in. What can be done about them?

We demand that sex work be decriminalised. This does not mean establishing licenses. That creates a whole set of new complications: recognition from doctors and the police; the red tape of the law. That will aggravate corruption. By 'decriminalising', what we mean is this: if two people want to have sex by mutual consent, if this is in no way a nuisance to others, then it should not be questioned. This is particularly important in Kerala, where there are no brothels. I've visited brothels in many places as part of my organisational work. They are run best in Kolkata and in Karnataka. In these places they are acceptable, to a certain degree. In Mumbai and other places, there is often utter wretchedness. The brothels in Mumbai are the worst. The kind of brothels you find in Mumbai are simply, totally unacceptable. In Kolkata and Karnataka, sex workers in brothels have the power to choose their clients, fix the remuneration and the amount of time to be spent on each client.

Mumbai brothels are what people have mostly seen and heard about; that's the main reason why such a horrifying picture comes into most people's minds when they hear about brothels. There are many exaggerated images circulating about Mumbai's red light areas. Even educated people believe blindly in these. For example, there is the idea that sex work in the red light area is licensed. Certificates are issued there for health purposes; also there are certificates that indicate safe and unsafe areas. That's not licensing. Women are tortured in these places. They have no rights, no freedom, they have to submit to all those who are brought there. There are no brothels in Kerala. Till around twenty to twenty-five years back, there used to be 'Company Houses'.

Opposition came not just from the media and politicians, but also, sometimes unknowingly, from those who seemed to be on our side. In our early days, a theatre person from Thrissur did a play for us. It showed sex workers dying horribly painful deaths in destitution. Since I believe that what we need is not sympathy or compassion but acceptance, I had an argument with him over the play. Following this, some members of our organisation apologised to him on my behalf, claiming that I had insulted him. I held firm to my opinion: that it was he who had insulted sex workers. For some time, I even distanced myself from the organisation over this issue.

Except for a few like Jayashree, in general, feminists are reluctant to accept sex workers. I think that's because they cannot see that sex is a woman's need as well. When I became active in organisational work, many asked me whether sex wasn't a man's need, and whether fulfilling it was being true to feminism. I don't think this is true; sex is not just a man's need. Feminists aren't very different from ordinary women; that's why they ask this.

Sex work and sexual exploitation are two different things. It is the sex workers whom we bring together in our organisation. Some may have landed up in this trade through exploitation. But only those who have decided to stick to this trade for good can become part of our organisation. If a woman is found on the streets, the organisation first conducts a counselling session to find out whether she chose this trade or came into it by accident. We try to help those who want to move out. Even though we can't find them jobs, if it is a domestic issue, we extend our help.

The 'sex racket' has nothing to do with sex work. In rackets, women are kidnapped and sold to whoever the kidnapper chooses. It is a naked display of force. The person trapped in it will be given no consideration, either mentally or physically.

Sexual exploitation means that people take you away for their enjoyment and use you. It is often without your consent, or on the false promise of work or marriage. Sex rackets aren't like this. The torture in these rackets is even more appalling than in the Mumbai brothels. In brothels, even if it is for a selfish end, women's health receives some attention. In rackets, young girls are brutally used, without any discretion, without any consideration for their minds or bodies, without rest or health care.

This means that there is a difference between sexual exploitation and sex rackets. A person who suffers sexual exploitation may become a sex worker.

Though we don't subscribe to the much touted idea of 'rehabilitation', the organisation helps those who want to move out of the trade in many ways. When we talk of work as a 'profession', that doesn't mean that we always enjoy doing it. For example, take a construction worker. No one takes up that kind of work saying that it is enjoyable, and that one is doing it so that one can admire the beauty of the building slowly rising up! The fellow who does scavenging work for the municipality does the job for a living. Sex work is a little above these two kinds of work. These days, those who do construction work are not in a position to keep aside anything for the future. In contrast, if sex workers are given the freedom to work, they need to work only three days a week to make a regular income, and remain healthy. No one demands the rehabilitation of scavengers who work under the unhealthiest conditions, since that will cause the whole place to stink. Fellows who are out to pinch and prod women on the sly give out exactly the same stink. This is not something that safeguards the health of society.

Buy Sex?

Some writers have been asking — isn't sex an elevated experience, to be enjoyed with sensitivity, can it be *sold*? We are taught, 'The treasure of knowledge is the greatest of treasures.' Now, if we ask the teacher to give us this wealth of knowledge for free, will he do it? No. He needs a salary. He's accepted teaching as a livelihood precisely for that reason. Yesudas[1] does accept a fee for his wonderful singing; is that because music is not an enjoyable art? Sex should also be treated like that. The same sort of problems that plague other kinds of work are present in sex work as well. Just as the singer preserves his voice and his health, so must the sex worker. So what's the great sin if the sex worker asks for remuneration?

The word *veshya* comes from Sanskrit. It means 'she who seduces'. It's because it was reduced to an abusive term that we've had to find a new term: 'sex worker'. In my view, it's the insulting connotations that make all the difference; otherwise the words have the same meaning.

---

[1]   A popular singer in Kerala, K.J. Yesudas.

Sex work does not connote only sex. Buying sex may just be limited to a caress. It can be between people of the same sex, and not just between those of the opposite sex. I know many who tax their brains trying to figure out how lesbians can have feelings for each other. That sort of question should never be asked. Love, care, comforting — trying to assess how much of this is physical and how much is mental, is a barren exercise. People who try to calculate physical presence, mental presence, and social acceptance in sex in kilograms are to be pitied. When we say that the earth revolves around an axis, it is a concept. What is to be done if one starts insisting that its thickness and length should be accurately measured?

'Know through the eye': we often say. There's sex in seeing; in touching and caressing; and then there's deep, intense sex. These are all different.

We buy tape recorders and cassettes to listen to music. We also decide what kind of music to listen to. It's just the same as far as different kinds of sex are concerned. Those who are outside have no right to ask this question. They should ask themselves the question, 'Can sex be *bought*?' No one is saying that everyone should necessarily buy sex. Only those who want it need buy it. When we go to buy clothes, do we ever ask whether they can be sold? Do we ever say, 'We need clothes, please donate some?' All that needs to be ensured is that no rules are imposed on those who are prepared to sell or buy sex.

Besides, it isn't romance or devotion that's being sold at a price. A certain price is fixed for spending a certain amount of time with someone. We give the love and caring that people need. Instead of insisting that these shouldn't be sold, it is infinitely better to say that those who don't need it don't have to buy it. Those who say such things, don't they say, when it comes to their own affairs, that art is the very soul of humanity and that they lose themselves in it? Do these people dissolve themselves in art after taking the soul out of the body? If the soul goes out, the body's dead matter. That means this dissolving happens with the soul right inside the body. Like an injection — we inject something into the body.

'Quivering Cars'

A large number of my clients are people who come seeking advice about sex. Some of them want to find out how to keep an excessively eager wife happy. I tell them to find out by experience. How would I know? The only way for them to know is from each other. Maybe there's reluctance. One can well find out if one pays a little attention whether the other person likes to be touched in certain places or not; when they utter little protests; or when they keep quiet. When we take little kids to a shop, don't we figure out what catches their eye? Whether they are interested in chocolates or in *laddus*? It's people who can't manage to do this who come with questions. For many people, the chance to get to know each other in a relationship does not arise.

Why do we insist that all sexual relations should end in family ties? Do we have to wait till life-long relationships are forged, to know about real sex? Why do we decide that women are only for bearing and rearing children? What is wrong in accepting that lesbianism is family planning?[2] Lesbianism is actually family planning. The world doesn't need so many human beings. But if some are hell-bent on playing Brahma the Creator, let them!

It's very difficult to find a place to speak in private with those who come for advice. Sitting in the family room of a big hotel or in a park is one way out. But once you are known as a sex worker, this isn't easy. This leads to a lot of exploitation. Get into an auto rickshaw, and for a ten-rupee ride, you will be charged a solid seventy–five rupees. Go to a hotel where you can sit and talk in peace, and you'll have to keep on ordering food even when you don't want it. In some places, they hike up the bill. If you can manage to find a place to talk in a park or a bus stand, you don't have to bother about all this.

Suppose you check into a room in a lodging wanting more security. For a room for which you'd normally pay a hundred–and–fifty rupees, now you'd have to shell out no less than six hundred. If there were greater freedom to speak in public places, this huge expense would be considerably reduced. For many people, sex consists only of talking to each other.

Many people choose a bus journey for this. In Thrissur, people refer to 'quivering cars'. This refers to talking and having sex inside a car. The authorities even had the equipment to remove a car, using a crane! Nothing serious can happen to

---

[2] In Kerala, 'family planning' is the common way to refer to contraception.

people if cars on the wayside quiver a bit. Instead of taking it lightly, people blow the event up into a mountain, and spread rumours that 'there must be a bomb inside the car'! Bombs, indeed! And bombs that quiver and shake!

There are plenty of cars, vans and larger vehicles in town these days, which have curtains for the windows and other arrangements, but they are murderously expensive. The quivering of the cars becomes an issue when they are parked in secluded areas. On busy city roads, it isn't a problem. Recently, I had such an experience, in a car. This was with a client who usually refused to wear a condom, no matter how much you tried to persuade him. That day he agreed to use one. I thought he must have taken part in an AIDS awareness class. The reason, however, was simple. He was afraid the seat would get messed up.

We consider our homes to be the most private of all spaces. People tend to barge in even there. Even when there's mutual consent, it is depicted as sexual exploitation.

Ask any sex worker, and you're sure to find out that not all clients approach us for physical sex. Most clients come for advice or to talk. It is those who have fled society who come for physical sex.

Now, consider the famous temple festival of Thrissur, the world-renowned Pooram. It is, of course, famous for its marvellous fireworks. However, the fireworks aren't all for Pooram. There's the morning worship, the *sheeveli* and a lot of other rituals that follow. It all culminates in fireworks, that's all. Many of the sex workers' clients, however, are in the habit of beginning with the bang, with the fireworks, and leaving soon after.

Many construction workers, home nurses and so on also do sex work. In many of Kerala's cities, it is the construction workers who usually move into sex work. They have to bed with the supervisors to get work. If they don't, then the next day, someone else will report for work instead. Most of them move solely to sex work realising that they then don't have to do both construction work, which brings in poor wages, *and* sex work. That way, they have better earnings, too.

Money

I never haggle in money matters. I just accept whatever is asked for. After all, I got into sex work because I didn't stop to quibble when my mother-in-law demanded five rupees a day to bring up my kids.

There was nothing else I could have done in those days. There was no possibility of finding a rented house. I had to become part of a Company House in order to survive. Within a year of my husband's death, it was clear that this couldn't be. Apart from my brother and father, every man there wanted me. So I didn't waste much time thinking it over.

Even before this, I was keen on making money. Usually, everyone goes to the clay mine from Monday to Saturday. Sunday's work was extra; it usually involved mixing the clay in the mine. That fetched double the usual wages. So I used to really like going to work on Sundays. That money used to be spent in buying blouses. Work in the clay mine really spoilt our blouses. We had to wear mostly torn or darned ones. Then whatever extra money I could save, I used to spend on buying sweet-meats for my little sisters. The one just younger than me was eight years my junior. I had three little sisters. Seeing myself as someone who took care of the kids: that's the satisfaction I used to get from spending that way.

Later, I paid a hundred rupees a day to the woman who cared for my kid. That was a big sum then. I used to earn close to two hundred rupees per day, those days.

I studied a bit of Tulu when I was in Mangalore. Also, a bit of Kannada. Since I became familiar with Tulu, Kannada became unnecessary. After I left Mangalore and married Shahulkka, we lived in many parts of Tamil Nadu, and I picked up Tamil really well. After Malayalam, Tamil is the language I've used most. I love the style of Tamil orators and try to follow it.

It was Rajiv Gandhi's death that made me learn to read Tamil. Shahulkka read out that news to me. I didn't make it out too well. Tamil was also the language my girl learned. If I asked them something, these two wouldn't give me clear answers. That made me determined to learn, and I began to work at my girl's books.

There are many sorts of people among sex workers. There are high-society people, middle class, and low class folk. There are people who work for ten or fifteen rupees. There are also people who take a thousand rupees for an hour.

We don't count the most privileged in this group as sex workers. They are able to shield themselves from public view and so don't have to endure much suffering. They may have to suffer at the hands of some clients, that's all. Middle class sex workers usually also do some other kind of work. It is the lowest class that suffers most. It's they who get arrested by the police, beaten up by thugs. They are the ones who are forced to own up to all the filthy jobs done by pickpockets and criminals. Even when there's a murder, they are picked up on the charge of being in touch with the murderer.

Recently, when a man was found murdered at the Ernakulam boat jetty, because a used condom was found close to him, the inference was that a sex worker had been with him. On this excuse, sex workers were targeted. The police and society are not interested in seeking out the actual murderer. It's easy to lay the blame on sex workers. In the Thrissur market too, a similar case is going on.

There are many factors involved in deciding the degree of freedom one has with a client. The area from which one is operating is one of the most important. I have operated from almost all areas. Those who stand near the Thrissur KSRTC bus stand are considered the lowest class. The District Hospital is very close to this, but those who hang around there get VIP treatment. If, by any chance, you happen to meet a client near the KSRTC stand and start laying out your conditions to him, immediately the comment will follow that you're playing high-hat despite being low class. The same conditions can be easily put forward by a woman standing by the District Hospital. I have had both experiences early in my career, so I don't negotiate with clients in either of these places. I talk to them away from these places, and then I am able to talk frankly. I mean about the kind of sex allowed, the time stipulated, and so on.

If you stand near the Saktan stand, you're sure to be taken as utter low class. Doesn't matter what you look like. Your standard depends on the area you hang around in. Even if it's a regular client, these prejudices are sure to surface in their dealings if you are picked up at the wrong place.

The client's social standing also affects the way he behaves. If the client is an auto rickshaw driver, very often we go out with him thinking that he's going to be quite terrible. But, it often happens that these characters turn out to be mild and don't insist on having an obnoxious this or that in sex. It's true however that one has to be selective. Middle class men are usually set on getting their money's worth in physical sex. But the better-off fellows, especially if they are young, are often violent and brash. They like to bulldoze you and get what they want. And no matter how affectionate you are towards them, it's the same. That's one of the reasons why I refuse to have clients of that age.

I took my first steps in this trade wearing the traditional Malayalee sari, the *settu-mundu*. Because the gold-bordered *settu-mundu* looked rather ostentatious, I preferred the black-and red-bordered ones. But this means a lot of bothersome work, starching and ironing. That's how I began to wear the regular sari. Those days, I never had a chance to check whether my blouse was a matching one, or whether it was cut in the latest fashion. I'd wear a sari with any blouse, that was it. The blouses I wore with any sari were largely black or red, something that I carried over from my *settu-mundu* days. When I started wearing saris, I decided against silk. That was because I believed they were exclusively for weddings. I also did believe that I was beautiful, if I had a bath and smeared sandal paste on my forehead.

During my days in the clay mine, I wore a *lungi* and a blouse. There wasn't much of a choice in dressing up, those days. Wear a white *mundu* when you go out; wear a coloured or spotted one when you go to work — that was the general rule everywhere.

Sex workers are exploited mainly by brokers and 'husbands'. Many of the latter are brokers. Irrespective of whether they work or not, they have to be supplied with liquor and money. Just like us, these people are also held in contempt by society. In Kozhikode, there is even a name for them: 'ropers'. Rope, of course, is used to tie up two ends. He who acts as a rope is the 'roper'.

These men are also the reason why sex workers have more than one child. Most sex workers use condoms. But not with these fellows who play the role of husbands. And these chaps are never stable. They stick with you for a year or two. Then there'll be another husband, and the pressure to have his kid. And the sex worker ends up with more kids than she wants. These fellows are useful when it comes to such things as renting out a house. But overall, they are a nuisance.

My parents weren't the type who uttered obscenities. I happened to be exposed to such language a bit in the colony near our house. That wasn't outright vulgar language. Well, it was something that could be heard in the presence of Father and Mother.

There was some progress in this regard at the clay mine. There they spoke foul things, but in words with double meanings, and so it didn't sound smutty right away. It was when I fell out with Rosa *chechi* and began to hang around the Thrissur round that I really heard first-rate coarse language. It's the women who rest in the streets after begging for alms and sex workers who are liberal in their use of crude language for the sake of security when lying in the streets. If the fellow who's harassing you has a shred of decency left, he'll withdraw quickly when his father and mother are showered with choicest abuse. But if the fellow is worse — a hoodlum — he'll give it back in the same coin. And this rain of uncouth words ensures that the police won't enter that place.

In towns, one can hear abuses being spat out in dark corners almost all the time. It's not just sex workers who do this. Pungent tongues are also the sole defensive weapon that married couples from Tamil Nadu, who come here seeking work, have. They are still very much used precisely because they effectively repel any assailant who has some sense of honour left in him.

That doesn't mean that all sex workers are foul-mouthed. Actually the foul-mouthed ones are rare. But people are still prejudiced; they believe that sex workers are all foul-mouthed, and that only sex workers use such language.

Some of the people high up in society have told me, 'You

don't look like a *veshya* at all.' When low-down characters want to say the same thing, they say, 'You don't look like a *petti*.'

I have always felt that the word *petti* is highly insulting; it pushes you to the margin. The word *veshya*, however, seems to indicate merely where one stands, and what one does. Like we call the woman who does the reaping a 'reaper', it isn't wrong to call a woman who does sexual seduction a *veshya*. But words like *petti* and *tatti* are used with the worst sort of contempt.

There's a joke about the word *petti* — which means a 'box', literally — that comes to my mind. Someone from Thrissur went to Guruvayur. He did some shopping there and soon needed a box to store the things he'd bought. He hailed an auto rickshaw and asked the driver to take him to a place where he could get a good *petti* — a box. The chap brought him to the east gate of the temple where we used to hang around. There you can see many sex workers. The fellow who needed the box looked around — no shops anywhere close!

'Why've you stopped near the road? I thought I told you to take me to a shop.'

'*Saar*, there's the *petti*, over there. Tell me which one you want. I'll get her in here.'

'What the hell — I need a *petti*!'

Now the auto rickshaw driver was utterly confused. 'What do you really want, *saar*?'

'Hey, I've done a lot of shopping; I need a box to carry all that stuff.'

The auto chap went red in the face. It's he himself who told me this story, at great length!

When the police fired on the tribals at Muttanga, a large convention was held in protest at Manantavadi, and I also took part in it. I went there because I was invited. When I was called to speak, a young girl came up to the mike and announced loudly that Janu[3] and a sex worker were not to be treated alike. It was clear that someone had made her do that. I didn't want to create trouble in those circumstances, and so I got up and declared that I wasn't going to speak. This experience was a good eye-opener with regard to the prejudices that even highly motivated political activists lug around. The police *lathi*-charged the many protest demonstrations organised around that incident. A state-wide general strike was declared against this the next day, which made my journey back difficult. I managed to hitch a ride on some vehicle and reached Kozhikode by evening. Those who were with us went to their friends' houses. An activist of the women's organisation, Sakhi, and I were left. We stayed in the office of another women's organisation, Anveshi. That woman was very restless. She didn't sleep a wink that night. Only the next morning did I find out why. She was scared that I, being a sex worker, would filch her bus fare to Thiru/ananthapuram if she fell asleep!

Jwalamukhi was started in the PSH project office. When the project ended after two years, our organisation also came to a stop. Then we opened offices at Ernakulam and Thiruvananthapuram.

---

[3] C.K. Janu, the woman-leader of the tribal struggles in Kerala.

It's not easy to find space for an office. People would not rent out their buildings even for the PSH project. Maitreyan really had a hard time looking for office space. Finally, he had to use his personal connections to find us a space. The rich and the poor are equally unsympathetic to us, in this matter. Maitreyan rented out a place close to a Dalit colony in Thiruvananthapuram, as a resting place for sex workers who have to wander the streets all the time. But that didn't last long. The argument that the poor would understand us better than the rich didn't seem to hold much steam. Apparently, the fear was that the dark-skinned women of that area would all be mistaken for sex workers, and so we were asked to shift to a better locality. When it was pointed out that this problem wouldn't arise in a better-off area, we had to give in. We vacated the house.

Paulson's personal connections helped us in building the organisation at Kozhikode, too. A police officer, a relative of his, was very helpful in keeping police interference minimal.

In Jwalamukhi, however, a sense of community was more important than personal connections. Because we were all from different places and dependent upon the PSH project, Jwalamukhi was more democratic.

My very first documentary was *Jwalamukhikal*. The second one was *Nisabdarakkapettavarilekku Orettinottam (A Glimpse of the Silenced)*. This was about police atrocities. Besides capturing the experiences of sex workers, it had interviews with an advocate, a doctor, a police officer and an auto rick-shaw driver. Seven women and five men were interviewed. I asked all the questions myself.

After I returned from Thailand, we organised camera workshops for sex workers. In my first workshop, I was helped by Sajita, Reshma, Gopakumar and others.

After Thailand, my documentaries were screened in Thiruvananthapuram by the Russian Cultural Society and at the international festival of films on sexual minorities in Mumbai. In Mumbai, I was given VIP treatment as the director of a documentary. I was invited as a guest on the TV channel, Asianet's News Hour, when it was shown in Thiruvananthapuram.

Now I'd like to work on a feature film, independently.

If I'm sad, I like to have a drink by myself. But if I'm happy, I need company for a drink. And then I like the chance to argue and be defiant.

I started drinking with Subbarettan and used to drink hard and well. When we sold hooch, I met many drunkards. I saw that many became extra-affectionate towards their families once they got drunk. There was a boy who used to come there; I took a liking to him. He never had the guts to go beyond light brushes. I used to want him at times.

Even the terrible thug Manali Parameswaran was scared of Subbarettan. He'd come, drink his fill in silence and leave.

Even when I used to drink regularly, I never became a slave to it. I've never taken things to the extent that not drinking would bring me a headache. In everything — whether it's drinking, sleeping, eating or travelling — I always adopt a style that's affordable, that I can have without depending on anyone else.

These days several people advise me to give up the habit. I've also made promises about kicking it to those who are dear to me. But I can't really stop drinking for them!

To think that one must deny oneself pleasure while working to build an organisation is a prejudice. Many take it for granted that I make money and therefore I am irresponsible. That's because I'm lazy. There's no need for sacrifices; all things can be done. We curl up in our laziness, deciding that this is all we can do, and no more.

In 2003, we held the Festival of Pleasure at Thiruvananthapuram, and it caught public attention. The police firing at Muttanga happened around that time, and we changed its name to Festival of No Pleasure. Sex workers, people with same sex preferences and eunuchs from all over India took part in it. Delegates from fourteen foreign countries attended the event paying airfares on their own. Rejecting the charges that such events were funded by foreign agencies, we made public our accounts, putting them up in the open near the conference site.

A controversy was sparked off by this event too; some charged that it was organised by middle class intellectuals. The Festival of Pleasure was a coming-together, as a community. We did have a few people helping us in this. Maitreyan helped us to send the emails and to draft statements in English. Does that mean that he taught us sex work? Was I not a sex worker before I met him? We didn't turn sex work into pleasure there. The pleasure was in sex workers and non-sex workers sharing a common platform. We were always cast out from society. To have a space which we could share with others, this was the pleasure we enjoyed there.

People who complain like this want everything just to themselves, a monopoly. As if only they can think and talk of such things! Sex workers have always bedded people with a good education. They can understand the language they speak, and the things they speak of. We also gain a certain knowledge from intellectuals. Sex workers go to bed not only with workers but also with businessmen and policemen. A sex worker is not born as a sex worker's daughter. These are women who come into the trade after having failed their higher secondary school exams, after failing to get a job, or after being kicked out by a husband irked at having got only thirty thousand, instead of the fifty thousand promised, as dowry. There are school teachers among us. What more is there that they can be taught?

***

It was after the PSH project that the word 'pick-up point' began to be used. Once we became participants in the PSH project, we were nicknamed 'condom teachers'. The Women's Society formed in Bangladesh Colony was registered under the Charitable Societies Act. It consisted of only sex workers. It took up sexual health awareness programmes, the distribution of condoms and other health issues. There's a small stipend for those who work as peer educators among sex workers. The major problem was the refusal to wear condoms by clients. The name 'condom teacher' was, of course, in recognition of our efforts to raise awareness regarding the use of condoms.

***

It was at Mangalore that I met a man waiting for male clients for the first time. It was like seeing an alien creature. This was twenty-seven years ago. Sulaiman had made up his face just like a woman; he was also a broker for women sex workers. When I met him as a broker, I found out that there were many others like him.

Now I know many such people who are part of our work. Today in Kerala, there are more male sex workers than female sex workers.

CHAPTER SEVEN

Men, Now and Then

There's a special reason why most of my clients come to me for advice. There are few among us who are willing to speak for a long time with clients. But when I see a client getting tense, I usually ask him what the matter is. Some people don't want sex once they are inside the room. They keep asking us about our life and habits. That's to open up a conversation. I then ask what the real problem is. Gradually I began to get more and more clients who wanted to talk. Some men would come to me and say, my friend told me, you'll get sound advice from *chechi*. These are often men about to be married. There are also others whose marriages have failed. It's these two types that want advice, mostly.

Many men in their mid-forties with their marriages in shambles have come to me with complaints. There's one man who told me that he gave his wife a lot of love, helped with washing the dishes, with washing the clothes, but she didn't want him in bed at night. In such cases, I ask for more details about their relationship and usually the problem is easy to locate. The women in such cases generally expect greater sexual skill and experience from their men. And in turn, these men never admit to ignorance if the wife points it out. 'Who taught you all this?' That would be the question! So even if the wife can make out what's wrong, she can't tell him. If he doesn't know, he's not going to ask either.

I've also had another interesting experience. A person came to me once, wanting advice. He told me he was forty-two years old. He was married at twenty-six. 'So,' I asked, 'what were you doing all this time?' 'How is one to ask one's wife about these things?' he replied.

After the AIDS awareness campaigns, many people have new problems. We keep hearing about safe sex. What's that? Is there any method apart from the condom? Of course, in our society, the idea that sex must end in a blast of fireworks is a must! Some say, 'I'm pretty content with the early worship, but my wife doesn't agree.' If you ask the wives, they'll tell you just the opposite. People have no clue about where the problem starts, where it ends — or whether it really has a beginning and end in a fixed way at all!

Some do come back to tell me all about it, if my advice works. There's a chap from Shornur. He must have been about thirty then. He learned all his lessons from me. Then he came up to me one day and said, 'Chechi, when I see you next, I'll act like a stranger.' Apparently, things had become all right between him and his wife.

There's another man, a certain Prakashan. When I told him about my plans to write an autobiography, he insisted that I must put in his name. He's a hotel manager and quite well-off. His first wife left him because she wasn't happy with their sex life. He came to me when he was about to remarry, after the marriage had been arranged. He was very fond of his first wife. But they would quarrel at night. He told me to include his name in my book after we'd discussed all that.

Then there was the man from Kollam who was a neighbour of Mata Amritanandamayi. He wanted to meet her, but as she'd been his neighbour, he didn't believe she had wondrous powers. So he came to me. Once he'd talked with me, he decided that I had some divine power. Imagine — just because Amritanandamayi happened to be his neighbour, it was I who became divine! Such a bizarre leap of logic!

Very few of these people come to me by chance. Most of them come looking for me after getting to know of such a *chechi* from others. I've told you about people who like to travel together with us in buses. Some of them are scared that sex workers might rape them if they find themselves alone in a room with any of us!

I had an unusual relationship with someone called Asokan who ran a hotel in the Chettiyangadi area of Thrissur. At night, his hotel doubled as a place where people gambled at cards. He used to like to lie with me in one part of the hotel while his friends played cards in another. Later I heard from someone else that he had committed suicide.

When I lived near Amala in Thrissur, there was a person called Ibrahim who used to take me to his house in his Maruti Zen. His wife and kids would be home then. He'd raise the shutters leaving me inside the car, park the car inside the shed and go in. After everyone was asleep he'd come out, at around midnight. All this, without a trace of fear. Around three, he'd drop me back home in the car.

A lorry driver from Amballoor, Paramu, loved to show off his machismo by seating me in his lorry and driving right through the city centre.

Recently, I met a medical representative. A bug-eyed chap, quite bald except for some scanty hair sticking out from here and there, with a big bracelet on one arm, a watch, a red thread – quite a clown, I must say. A bit like the pompous ass of a police officer in the Malayalam movie *Sanmanassullavarkku Samadhanam*! He liked to give the impression of being a big macho man. He was the sort who liked travel sex, that is, travel in a luxury bus, touch, caress, talk a little – that's all he needed for sex. If it were in a train, it would be freer; one could hug and kiss better.

I met this man for the first time some five or six months back at Thrissur. It was a time when things were a bit tight, financially. I had made a round of the railway station and just come into the bus stand when he came right behind me and said, 'Get into this bus.' Since we hadn't fixed an amount, I hung back, doubtful. Right then, another fellow came up and began to talk to me as if we were old friends. I saw that this second fellow was a trickster; he'd fudge when it came to the cash. I made an excuse to go to the toilet to get rid of him, but when I returned, there this chap was again. He asked me whether I'd go with him to Ernakulam. 'What about the money?' I asked. 'How much?' he wanted to know. 'Three hundred,' I said. 'I'll get it now,' he said, and left. I stood there wondering where he'd gone for the three hundred. I realised only later that he meant he would have to get the cash out of his suitcase!

And so we finally got into the bus. No action at all, from his side. He sat there through the journey like a good boy. 'You can go to sleep if you feel like it,' he said. After some time, he took out three hundred rupees and held it out to me. My cell phone rang as he was doing this. After I took the call, he asked for my number and took it down.

When we got off, he walked for some distance, turned and gave me a glance. He probably thought I would go with him. He came back to me and said, 'Take care to eat well, okay?' 'I'll do just what I please with your cash,' I whispered in my mind. Then he took out another hundred, folded it and gave it to me. He walked on for some distance, turned back again, took another peek at me, and then went straight off. He told me to put down all the details except his name when he got to know I was writing this.

In earlier times, clients liked us to act like wives. They'd want us to wash their towel, hand them the soap, walk behind them lugging their suitcase. But if there was anything valuable inside the suitcase, since they were scared that we'd make off with it, they'd turn around every now and then to check whether we were still there. I used to be most amused by this. Think of it — giving someone a box to carry, and then worrying to death whether that person would run away with it!

Others would be worried whether we'd slip away, and would instruct us to follow them closely and not be tempted by other people's offers. They always walked with their nerves stretched, expecting us to disappear any moment. Irrespective of whether the sex turns out to my liking or not, I really love these journeys. Even if you've been with such men a thousand times, there's no change in their attitude: 'I'm a respectable individual; you are a whore.' They never arrive at the realisation that they are clients. This insufferable attitude was what made me leave sex work at one point and become an ordinary housewife. There's not much difference in this between the best and worst of clients.

In those days, it was difficult to hang around the railway station or the bus stand at night. These men knew that women would put up with anything, because of this. The police didn't think it was their job to poke their noses into sex workers' affairs. It was easy to nab us in public places, easy to beat us up in public places. If a woman was taken away by force from the KSRTC station, no one would ask any questions. Now a days things have changed somewhat. The police interfere now. Not to rescue the woman, but to establish their power, as if they are our protectors.

In the days of my youth, men had certain rights, they could touch and feel women's bodies. That used to be nothing more than a bare brushing or a trivial caress. It would not go beyond this and suddenly reach the bedroom. Compared to those times, things are bad now. The attitude these days is that women can be used in any way.

There's no concern for age. I used to ask Mother whether she didn't have problems travelling by herself. 'Mother's grown old, dear,' she'd say. She was around forty or forty-five then and quite pretty. Compared to that, I, in my fifty-second year now, am not safe. Anywhere I go, I get fondled, and by men of all ages. Men these days are more randy than men twenty-five years ago. Once when I was riding on a bus in Guruvayur, I felt a hand on my back busy fondling me. When he continued to bug me, I turned around. A very respectable gentleman, complete with a grand moustache. 'Don't take so much pain to stroke me here,' I loudly announced, 'tell me where you'd like to go. You can stroke me all you please there!' He blanched, and with a stupid smile plastered all over his face, stepped back.

My first journey to Thailand convinced me that things aren't very different on a plane. I was completely engrossed in the thrill of my first flight when my neighbour's finger went to work on me. He was sitting all covered in a blanket. I first thought he had done it by mistake. But when it happened again, I could make out what his disease was. I caught hold of his arm and firmly moved it away. Time has flown, but still no one tries to look at women as fellow-creatures and beings that can demand sex from them! They view sex as a right they can demand from any woman.

When I accept my clients, I always consider their age. I'm loath to have sex with people who are too young. Ten years my junior, that's my limit, not more. If you go out with someone thinking he's thirty-two, it sometimes turns out that he isn't that old. Recently something like that happened. A twenty-four-year-old took me out. He looked older than that. When we were there, he asked me, 'How old are you, *chechi*?' 'Forty-eight,' I told him; then he told me he was only twenty-three. I noted that he wasn't one bit bashful when he heard my age. In the older days, if a thirty-year-old man got together with a woman of thirty-five and came to know, he'd throw up his hands and declare that he preferred a younger woman. Those days, we always used to reduce our age by a year or two. Nowadays, even if we are double their age, there doesn't seem to be a problem. Before, a man would take only a woman who looked about the same age for a bus ride. She had to look like his wife at first glance, that was it. Now, there's no need for this.

These days, many prefer older women. Men like to talk about sex these days. That wasn't the case earlier; talking was rare. You go somewhere, shed whatever you're wearing around your waist, and well, that was all to it.

Another change is in the men who come all prepared after watching blue films. They think it's possible for people to go on and on for thirty minutes. Of course, they point out that the film they watched had lasted thirty minutes! And of course, it's not they who are at fault, it's all our inadequacy! It's the middle-aged folk who act this silly. The youngsters aren't as bad.

'Memory, Alive and Clear'

An Interview with Nalini Jameela

Interviewed by **J. Devika**, August 2007.

'I am a sex worker among the intellectuals' — that is how you described yourself recently, in response to a barbed comment that 'Nalini is now the intellectual among sex workers' — is that a comment on your life after the publication of your autobiography in Malayalam?

Well, my response was intended as a protest against a certain way of labeling that irritated me no end. If you remember, I had made a short film a while ago. What did many people say? 'A sex worker has made this film', or 'a village bumpkin has made this film', or 'an uneducated person...', and so on. It was not even 'a woman has made this film'! When they say that 'a sex worker has made this film', they try to define me only as a sex worker. This was my way of throwing their phrases back at them.

After the publication of my book (in Malayalam), I found that this sort of labeling became worse, especially within Kerala. Outside, however, I have gained a lot of respect. I have been working recently in Mysore and Andhra Pradesh — in both places I was treated well, on equal footing with doctors, for example. Many years ago, when I was part of Jwalamukhi, the sex workers' organisation, everybody was fond of me. Of course, during those days I was in the position of someone who needed 'rescuing'! As long as you are in a place where you're asking for help, constantly crying, 'Save me, help me!' people care about you. The minute you pick yourself up and stop crying for help, the sympathy stops flowing! In fact, the crying gives them a kick — they don't like it when you stop giving them that pleasure! If you keep on crying, many will rush to your rescue — but that's just for a short while.

I'm not upset that many people who were once close now run away from me these days — their fear seems comic! Another thing that seems funny to me — I'm often asked why I wrote about my story in the book, instead of including the stories of my suffering sister-sex workers. This question makes two false assumptions. First, I have written about other sex workers and their sufferings — so the real complaint is that I have also included my own story! I tell them that it's my autobiography; it will have more of my story. When I say this, what they hear worries them: this isn't the voice of the woman screaming, 'Help me, help me!' Second, this question makes the assumption that I have not suffered in my experiences with sex work! It's a neat set of traps, don't you think?

***

In your book, i was struck by the way, in the Malayalam version, you seem to talk of the past in the present tense...

That's the way my memory is. I remember my past in moving pictures, like a film, with scenes that are sharp in my mind. My very first memory, the one where my grandmother is crawling towards us... I can clearly see her elongated earlobes dangling as she came up. Perhaps it's also because of the kind of past I've survived — every step in my life has been a grim battle. At each stage, I'd look back at the danger that I had escaped. Often I would marvel at how I survived, and then I would relax, once I'd seen that all it took to overcome apparently insurmountable difficulties was a little effort. I suppose it's the habit of looking back so frequently that has kept my memory alive and clear.

I have always drawn strength from my memories in troubled times. After the first shock when trouble descends, I take a moment to reflect on all the challenges I have survived. If I could go through all that, I tell myself, why be scared now? Have I not reached greater heights in my life through all my troubles, have I not fulfilled my responsibilities, become a mother and a grandmother, why should I lose heart now? Also, I constantly draw energy from my past when I talk to other women about the trials in their lives.

Some people have made this observation in the form of a complaint, a much larger complaint, that what they hear in my autobiography is not my voice, but the voice of 'someone else'. They say that I use words like 'client' when I describe the past, though the word 'client' only came into general use far more recently. But we did use the word 'client' long before sex worker activism began, in a different way — it was part of our code language. It was the private language of those of us in sex work, and it was used to cover up what we did. It was when I became a social worker that I realised words like 'client' had a different meaning — one that had nothing to do with covering up the truth.

* * *

The shift from being an abused daughter-in-law to being a full-time sex worker must have been a significant one in your life — could you tell me more about that?

To tell you the truth, I didn't think of it at all. I had to go along with someone, he would pay me, and that was the end of it. I never thought I'd take up sex work as my means of livelihood. Never thought I'd fall into it, but I did. It wasn't a well-thought-out decision. But once I got into it, I decided to stand firm, to face all the problems and dangers with courage. And I hoped to rise above all my troubles some day. I often see young sex workers who are beautiful, but bowed and bent because they bear the huge burden of guilt. These are the young women who are most vulnerable to exploitation. I tell them, 'Once you get into this, it is important to pick yourself up. Stop pitying yourself, hold your head high; tell yourself, "This is where I am" and get a hold on your situation if you don't want to be exploited.'

Sex work changed my day-to-day life in many ways. My early life had been so difficult, so painful, that I rarely took the time to look good. But once I became a sex worker, I had to pay attention to my body. I began to dress well. That made me feel good — and gave me the confidence to accompany anyone, however high his status might have been! Paying attention to my body certainly helped me — I felt more cheerful, confident and more active. I saw that I could actually make an impression on a man. That doesn't mean making a client of him, getting him into bed — it means that you exert an influence on people. The man is aware of your presence; he can't ignore you.

My daily routine became more disciplined. In the company house you have to wake up early at dawn, bathe and dress so that you look fresh when clients come. At a later stage, when I met clients in hotels near temples, again, I had to be an early riser. In those places, you have to leave your hotel room at five in the morning to create the impression that you're going to the temple for the early morning puja.

It was hard to stay in touch with the few close women friends I had before I became a sex worker. Their husbands didn't want us to meet, but when they came to town, to see a movie, for instance, and passed by the places where I waited for clients, they would secretly get away to talk to me. Inevitably, at some point, they would ask me why I had to do this thing, and whether I couldn't give it up. That came out of distress — I was missing from their lives. They were also concerned that these men were 'doing things' to me. I would console them: they didn't have to worry about me, because I had good friends, and well, the 'things' that my clients did to me were almost the same as the 'things' their husbands did to them!

* * *

You entered sex work in troubled times — during the Emergency. How did you, as a sex worker, experience the Emergency? You mention your close association with policemen in your autobiography.

My first experience of the Emergency happened when I was standing right inside a police station! Something strange was happening that day. Everyone who came to the police station — even those who were just visiting other prisoners — was beaten up, badly beaten up. I was roughed up myself the first time I was arrested. The second time I was arrested — at the Puthukad police station — I realised that this was a deliberate way of terrorising ordinary people.

At Puthukad station, one of the policemen was a bad-tempered sort, notorious for his violent outbursts. I was worried — would I be beaten up by him too? But after that first experience of being beaten at the station, I had made sure that a few policemen became my clients. That wasn't very difficult. Besides, power in the police station doesn't depend on hierarchy: it doesn't begin with the circle inspector and sub-inspector and dwindle at lower levels. It's much more complicated. There are many policemen at junior levels who exert tremendous influence on their seniors. I knew that, and was careful to keep such men on my side. One of my policemen clients worked in this police station and so I turned to him for help. 'Don't worry,' he said, 'you won't be harmed, I have dropped a word in the circle inspector's ear already.' The bad-tempered policeman, who'd been hoping to take his anger out on me, was of course disappointed! I can still see him, mad with anger, rampaging like a brute of a dog straining at the leash!

The circle inspector said that while I would be spared a beating, I could leave the police station only in the care of a male relative. My policeman-client helped me find a suitable 'relative', a well-known local person who was a supervisor at a tile factory, and who posed as my cousin. He picked me up from the station, and we left unharmed. In those days, to emerge from the police station unharmed was for us ordinary people a matter of great pride! It seems very amusing today. In the middle of the terror of the Emergency, a man coming to collect a sex worker from the police station, and leaving unscathed — and that too, because of the woman's influence!

* * *

One of the most powerful aspects of your story is the way in which it highlights how, for marginalised women, the moral distinctions made between sex work, housework, and paid work are quite irrelevant...

People do all kinds of work in order to survive. The struggle to survive is largely the woman's burden — she's the one who has to find money for the children's upbringing, for health expenses, for parents. This applies to rich and the poor alike, though rich women may have more resources. But if your life is a struggle to survive and to support others, then you won't be concerned with whether the work you can get is dignified or not.

In order to find work and to keep a job, you have to please many people. A woman is expected to offer her body — many women have nothing else. And then she doesn't care about being the faithful wife. And 'dignified work'- like domestic work — is quite 'dirty' too; you have to clean up other people's messes, wash their dirty clothes. Nor is that the end of it. Men in homes where women work as domestic workers aren't concerned about this being 'dignified' work — many of them will pressure the woman working in their homes to do 'undignified' things! They are like snakes that lie in wait for the frogs, absolutely still — the frogs hop around, unaware, and are swallowed by the snakes in a flash!

It's not as if elite women don't know this; but it is convenient for them not to recognise this. They have much to gain if the divide between 'dignified' them and 'undignified' us stays intact. However, my co-workers in the sex workers' organisation know that the divide is very thin.

One must emphasise the meaninglessness of this divide over and over again, in different ways. Recently at a meeting, I was asked by a young woman journalist whether sex workers weren't harassed in the course of their work. This was what I said to her: 'There are two ways you can pluck a ripe mango. You can either strike it down the hard way, with a stone, or you can pluck it softly, handle it gently. In the end, the mango will be eaten, anyway!' Getting married is no safeguard against violence, even though the common consensus is that one can bear violence from a husband, but not violence from a client.

* * *

I found your detailed descriptions of your experience of mothering really moving. In the stereotypical accounts of sex workers' lives, such an account would be hard to come by...

You know what I think of that? One should never be one-dimensional. We often hear women who have, say, entered politics, and say that now there's no time to spend with the kids; we hear about film actresses, for example, who have given up careers to care for their families. I disagree with these women. It's like saying that one can do only one thing — when the meal consists of rice and curries, would you say that because you have to finish the rice, you can't eat the curries alongside?

I'm against that — I look after my family, I also do social work, and when in financial need, as someone in my situation often is, I do sex work. Life isn't a narrow, one-track path; there are detours one can take, and one can also return to old, familiar paths.

There are people who say that I'm not true to one vocation, and that somehow doing many things is linked to a craving for fame. I don't think this is true. As far as I can see, it is those who run after fame who care little for dependents and friends, and devote themselves to chasing their goals. When people choose to do many things, many of the things they do are often for the benefit of others.

On motherhood: there is really no separation between being a mother and being a sex worker. Of my daughters, the one I raised myself understands this well. But my older daughter, who was separated from me and knows little of my struggle, cannot see it. People prefer not to see our struggles to bring our children up — when some poor woman gets arrested and sentenced for sex work, she is separated from the children who must have been left in someone's care. When her prison term ends, often she has no way of reaching her children; she may not know where they are. And people will use this example to pillory us: sex workers don't care for their children! They don't see the agony; they don't recognise our sheer helplessness!

* * *

In your chapter on your clients, you seem to be almost 'writing resistance' — making that chapter an opportunity to resist the power of the client over the sex worker, primarily by laughing at him...

A client always speaks to you from a position of absolute power — long before he becomes your client. He sets the rules: you have to be with him for so much time; you have to do this, this, and this, and you'll get only so much money. I never oppose the client — in fact, I am soft, mild, I half-agree, half-disagree with his demands, and gradually bring him around to abide by to the things I will not do. By the end of this, he is usually mine. From then on, I set the rules! I decide where to go, which hotel, what food and liquor to order. I take away his power from him, subtly.

Women get into trouble when they don't follow a simple rule — never go where the client wants you to go. Very often, women who agree to go to the client's hotel room find that they are trapped. In that situation, a woman could be gang-raped, or tortured, or remain unpaid. But it is not always easy to avoid such situations. Even the strongest of women would find it hard to escape such a situation — you have to have your wits about you.

I have always made fun of my clients. My very first experience was with the policeman with whom I shared such a wonderful time — after which he had me arrested. That's when I realised that most clients don't want your affection. 'We don't care how much you care about us: we will remain distant masters,' that's what they think. After I got over the initial shock of realization, I began to show them that they weren't as powerful as they assumed, that they could be cut down to size. I have always found this amusing, and that's what you found in that chapter.

* * *

About the last chapter — many readers, including myself, felt that it was weak in many ways...

Yes, I agree. That was because I wanted to write this version of my autobiography in a hurry, to remedy the damage caused by the first, inadequate draft that was published. I was so concerned about reclaiming my autobiography that I really didn't have the time to think it through properly.

If I had another chance, my last chapter would be an appeal to my community — exhorting them to be less reticent, to enter public life, and be of service to the public, for the good of society. I would also have taken the chance to speak to girls from other communities, who are young and know little of life. They are the victims of sex rackets and I would have advised them on how to avoid such traps.

***

You took the bold step of reclaiming your autobiography — not an easy thing to do. Could you tell us how and why this happened?

There was uproar when I decided to rewrite my book. But even when the first version came out, many thought that I — and my story — were not true. They thought this was fiction, that I wasn't a real person. Before this controversy had died down, I decided to rewrite my book, and that created much upheaval. The story was that the person who helped me with the first version 'created' me, and then, because I am a woman, the 'feminists' stole me from him. Whichever way you see it, in this story, I'm like a puppet who dances to others' tunes!

I could do this — make the decision to rewrite — because I had many friends, men and women, who were young activists, of whom few are known to be 'feminists!' With them — N.Baiju,

Shaju V.V, Shameena P.V, Reshma Bharadwaj, S.Sanjeev, and Dileep Raj — I have had very equal relationships. We were friends — they didn't treat me as if I were an older sister or something. That was excellent, because when they agreed to help me write, it was clear that they wouldn't tell me how to write. They never pretended to be more learned than me; I never felt I was less learned than them. I could express myself in my own style with them. And they worked as a group, which was very good for me, since their many questions reactivated my memories and allowed me to tell a good story.

This wasn't the case with the first version. The person who worked with me didn't encourage the participation of others — it was only his effort that counted. And I hardly ever participated in shaping the story. Whenever I made a suggestion about the style, he'd tell me that this was not the way it was done, that the rules of an autobiography didn't allow it, or something else.

Let me also tell you that the struggle to get this story written the way I wanted it written, and to get it into the public eye, has been as intense as any in my whole life. A few chose to stand by me even when the going wasn't good. They could have given up on me, but they didn't, and I am truly grateful for such abundant friendship.

I should warn you that I might write again in the future — 'My autobiography, Part II'! As long as one's life continues to offer fruitful experiences that may cast light on other people's lives and sorrows, one should share what one can. For that reason, I will keep on telling you the story of my life.